About This Book

Why is this topic important?

Every day first line managers and supervisors struggle with deficiencies and inequities in their organization, their leadership, and their people. The book recognizes that deficiencies exist, yet focuses on those things that first line managers and supervisors can do to be more effective.

What can you achieve with this book?

The book serves as a working guide. It is full of proven, practical guidelines, tools, and tips to overcome deficiencies and inequities, whether they are in the organization, the leadership, or the employees. The guidelines and tools on the accompanying CD can be immediately put to use or modified to accommodate unique situations.

How is this book organized?

The book is organized around the four major roles of first line managers and supervisors. There are two chapters dedicated to each role. The first role is to *provide direction*. The chapters explain how managers and supervisors can provide direction whether or not they have been given clear direction themselves. The second role is to *communicate expectations*. The chapters explain how to identify behaviors that lead to results and how to measure performance. The third role is to *equip* people with skills, information, and tools so they can succeed. The chapters explain how to orient new people to the job, how to help them get the most from training, and how to make use of quick reference guides so people avoid mistakes and perform more consistently. The fourth role is about how to *steer* or keep people on course through feedback and incentives. The chapters explain how to take the pain out of giving people feedback and how to recognize and reward behaviors that produce results.

About Pfeiffer

Pfeiffer serves the professional development and hands-on resource needs of training and human resource practitioners and gives them products to do their jobs better. We deliver proven ideas and solutions from experts in HR development and HR management, and we offer effective and customizable tools to improve workplace performance. From novice to seasoned professional, Pfeiffer is the source you can trust to make yourself and your organization more successful.

Essential Knowledge Pfeiffer produces insightful, practical, and comprehensive materials on topics that matter the most to training and HR professionals. Our Essential Knowledge resources translate the expertise of seasoned professionals into practical, how-to guidance on critical workplace issues and problems. These resources are supported by case studies, worksheets, and job aids and are frequently supplemented with CD-ROMs, websites, and other means of making the content easier to read, understand, and use.

Essential Tools Pfeiffer's Essential Tools resources save time and expense by offering proven, ready-to-use materials—including exercises, activities, games, instruments, and assessments—for use during a training or team-learning event. These resources are frequently offered in loose-leaf or CD-ROM format to facilitate copying and customization of the material.

Pfeiffer also recognizes the remarkable power of new technologies in expanding the reach and effectiveness of training. While e-hype has often created whizbang solutions in search of a problem, we are dedicated to bringing convenience and enhancements to proven training solutions. All our e-tools comply with rigorous functionality standards. The most appropriate technology wrapped around essential content yields the perfect solution for today's on-the-go trainers and human resource professionals.

Pfeiffer
www.pfeiffer.com

Essential resources for training and HR professionals

Performance-Based Management

What Every Manager Should Do to Get Results

Judith Hale

Pfeiffer

www.pfeiffer.com

ISBN: 0-7879-6036-5

Library of Congress Cataloging-in-Publication Data
Hale, Judith A.
    Performance-based management : what every manager should
        do to get results/Judith Hale.
            p. cm.
    Includes bibliographical references and index.
    ISBN 0-7879-6036-5 (alk. paper)
    1. Management by objectives. 2. Performance. 3. Supervision of
employees. I. Title.
    HD30.65.H355 2004
    658.4'012—dc21   2003008893

Acquiring Editor: *Matthew Davis*
Director of Development: *Kathleen Dolan Davies*
Editor: *Rebecca Taff*
Senior Production Editor: *Dawn Kilgore*
Manufacturing Supervisor: *Bill Matherly*
Interior Design: *Joseph Piliero*
Cover Design: *Laurie Anderson*
Illustrations: *Lynn Kearny and Richard Sheppard*

Printing   10 9 8 7 6 5 4 3 2

Contents

NOTE TO READER: Wiley publishes in a variety of print and electronic formats and by print-on-demand. Some material included with standard print versions of this book may not be included in e-books or in print-on-demand. If this book refers to media such as a CD or DVD that is not included in the version you purchased, you may download this material at http://booksupport.wiley.com. For more information about Wiley products, visit http://www.wiley.com.

List of Figures

CD-ROM Contents

Preface

*T*his book is based on more than twenty-five years of experience witnessing managers and supervisors succeed despite inept leadership, ill-formed human resource policies, and inadequate information and communication systems. They succeeded because of their respect for others, their ingenuity in addressing problems, and mostly because of their unwavering optimism. I have immense respect for the people who live day-to-day with dysfunctional management systems. Geary Rummler said, "Put a good person in a bad system, and the system will win every time."[1] This may be true in many circumstances, but I see people succeeding in bad systems. This book is meant to help managers and supervisors become even more effective, whether they work in good or bad systems.

AUDIENCE FOR THE BOOK

The primary audience for this book is managers and supervisors who are responsible for:

- The performance of employees, contractors, suppliers, and third-party after-market partners
- Facilitating the successful deployment and adoption of major initiatives
- Evaluating recommended solutions to improving performance
- Working with others not in their chain of command

A secondary audience is internal and external consultants (human resource development, training and development).

The tips, guidelines, and tools are designed to be workable and practical so managers and supervisors can more effectively improve human performance.

ACKNOWLEDG-MENTS

Some very special people played a major role in helping make this book possible. They painstakingly read the first draft of every chapter and added insights, examples, and guidance. They are Deb Barrett, Training Manager; Ann Berasley, MBA; Mike Brogan, Manager of Organizational Development, Metropolitan Washington Airports Authority; Ann Daniels, Chipote Restaurants; Cordell Hauglie, Consultant, Delivery Systems Consulting & Training, Boeing; David R. Haskett, Manager, Instructional Design, Johnson Controls, Inc.; Jim Heine, Manager of Utility Services, Argonne National Laboratory; Nora Holcomb, Manager of Internal and External Training, CCG Information Systems; Roger Kaufman, Professor, Florida State University; Donald L. Kirkey, Learning & Development Manager—Global Operations, Johnson Controls, Inc.; Karen G. Kroczek, Manager of Technical Training, Plant Facilities and Services Division, Argonne National Laboratory; Dean R. Larson, Ph.D., CSP CEM CPEA, Department Manager, Safety & Industrial Hygiene, U.S. Steel—Gary Works; Annemarie Laures, Director, Learning Services, Walgreen Co.; Jim Momsen, Contractor, Instructional Designer; Gwendolyn Nichols-White, Implementation Manager, U.S. Cellular; Tom Norfleet, Manager of Corporate Services, Michigan Auto; Karen Preston, Director, Systems Support & Process Improvement Services, Performance Development Department, Walgreen Co.; George Pollard, Assistant Professor of Education and Director of Advance Programs, Crichton College; Joeli Ridley, Manager of Certification, Charles Schwab; Malou Roth, Consultant; Belinda Silber, Owner, Divanoir Catering; Kenneth Silber, Ph.D., Associate Professor, Educational Technology, Research and Assessment, Northern Illinois University; Mike Singleton, Holnam Industries; Charline Wells, Manager of Training and Performance, Sandia National Laboratory.

I was fortunate to have the continued confidence of Kathleen Dolan Davies and Matt Davis of Pfeiffer, whose support made this book possible. Special thanks goes to my friend Sue Simons, who continues to encourage me to be true to my style of simplicity and directness.

NOTE

1. This quote is from *Training* magazine (December 1986, p. 43.)

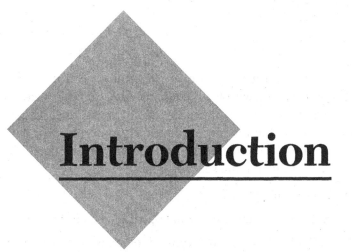

Introduction

*T*his book has stories, examples, and guidelines to help managers and supervisors improve the performance of their work units. Performance improvement operates on the premise that to be effective, individuals and groups require:

Direction About What the Organization Wants to Accomplish

- Consistent direction from the leadership
- Management processes that allow for efficient decision making

Clear Expectations

- A clear understanding of what is expected of them
- An explanation of the criteria that will be used to judge the adequacy of their work

The Equipment to Do the Job

- Training and the information required for the job
- Performance support tools to help them remember how to do the job right and efficiently

Information and Incentives to Keep Them on Track

- Feedback on how well they are doing and coaching on how to improve
- Rewards and incentives that support the behaviors that produce the results

Each of these requirements is discussed in greater detail in subsequent chapters.

FUNCTIONS OF MANAGEMENT

The functions of management are generally accepted as plan, staff, organize, and control along with lead, communicate, and motivate. The functions can be thought of as managerial duties and organizational processes. However you think of them, the functions, collectively, describe what has to happen for an organization to be competitive and to fulfill its mandate. These functions are based on a fundamental set of beliefs:

- Goals should be set
- Tasks can and must be planned, organized, and staffed
- Controls can and must be in place to assure that tasks are executed as expected
- Managers and supervisors can and must provide leadership, communicate the goals and plans, and motivate people to execute their tasks

However, the functions of management alone are not sufficient for people and organization to perform. To "perform" means to *deliver something of worth with integrity.* What you deliver is of worth if it contributes to society, the community, the organization, the customers, and the employees. Integrity is doing it without sacrificing environmental, social, or financial assets or relationships in the long run. Therefore, performance is about the ability to deliver on a promise while having the resiliency to withstand challenges, with few, if any, negative aftereffects. It applies to organizations, people, individually and collectively, systems, processes, products, and services.

PERFORMANCE IMPROVEMENT

Performance improvement is not a substitute for the functions of planning, organizing, controlling, leading, staffing, and so on. However, it imposes a perspective that questions the worth and worthiness of the effort, the results achieved, and the methods used. Planning, for example, is a process for setting goals or objectives; and plans are made up of strategies and tactics to accomplish the goal. Performance improvement questions the worthiness of the goal and the efficacy of the plan.[1,2]

Performance is about doing meaningful work in effective and efficient ways. Planning, organizing, controlling, leading, communicating, and motivating will help you do it. However, the management functions, in and of themselves, are not a substitute for maintaining focus, being grounded in the real constraints facing the organization, collaborating with people who have the resources, talent, and willingness to contribute to accomplishing the goal, and adding value to the overall effort. Just as the management functions presume work has to be organized with checks and balances in place, performance improvement presumes it is management's responsibility to do the following:

- Assure that where the organization is headed, what it does, and how it does it are appropriate considering the impact on society, the community, investors, customers, employees, and the competition

- Provide people with the direction, information, tools, materials, equipment, and appropriate rewards required for their efforts to produce the desired results

Performance improvement is a result-driven perspective to work, the workplace, and the worker. Recognizing the importance of organizing tasks and responsibilities, performance asks, "What are we about? What do we want to accomplish? What do people require to accomplish it? What are the best methods for providing what they require? What is the best way to motivate people so their efforts are more likely to produce the results we want?" And "What do we expect people to bring or contribute to the effort?" The principles of performance improvement advocate a collaborative and systematic approach to answering these questions.

Performance improvement is about what you do, why you do it, and how you go about it. A group performs when it achieves results in ways that are socially, environmentally, and economically prudent. Organizations, divisions, departments, work groups, teams, and individuals generate things that are used by someone else. If those things are not deemed valuable or have too high a social or economic cost, the people, individually and collectively, did not perform. When we say someone or something performs, we mean it delivers as promised.

Organizations perform when they produce goods and services that are valued by consumers and reap benefits to stockholders, but not at the expense of the environment, community, or employees. *Systems* perform when they support the information, communication, and transformation requirements of production and decision making, but not at the expense of other systems or departments. *Processes* perform when they generate products to a standard with minimal waste of time, money, materials, or human effort, but not if they operate as stand-alone silos that limit the effectiveness of other groups or processes. *People* perform when their efforts result in outputs that lead to positive short-term and long-term consequences.

PRINCIPLES OF PERFORMANCE IMPROVEMENT

Performance improvement, like management, operates from a fundamental set of beliefs or principles that include:

- Focus on results, keep the end state in mind, and do not become distracted
- Look at situations systemically, consider the larger picture, and identify ways to work effectively within constraints and competing objectives
- Add value to your people, your customers, and the organization now and in the future, because well-being and loyalty are critical to sustainable success
- Partner and collaborate with the appropriate groups and individuals, as success requires the expertise, understanding, and support of many people
- Be disciplined in how you approach and execute the work to be done, at minimum assess and analyze the facts, challenge assumptions, test out ideas, weigh alternatives, measure work in progress, and evaluate the results

Therefore, performance improvement is about staying focused on the right goals while dealing with real constraints and competing pressures, doing that which adds value, and collaborating with the right people. It is about being systematic and disciplined when you assess the situation, analyze probable causes, design and implement workable solutions, and evaluate whether what you did made a difference. Being proficient in both management and performance improvement is essential for personal and organizational effectiveness.

HOW THE BOOK IS ORGANIZED

The book has eight chapters that are organized around four main roles of the first line manager and supervisors (see Figure I.1).

Each chapter contains examples, guidelines, tools, tips, common missteps, and suggestions on where to learn more for each role. A CD-ROM disk containing all of the job aids and templates is found at the end of the book.

Role One: Provide Direction

Chapter 1: How Leaders Set the Direction. The goal of this chapter is to present ideas on how first-line managers and supervisors can stay help others stay focused on what matters. There are three tools in this chapter:

- Tool 1.1: How to Identify Goals and Objectives
- Tool 1.2: How to Identify What Is Important
- Tool 1.3: How to Challenge Mixed Messages

Figure I.1. Leadership Roles for Performance

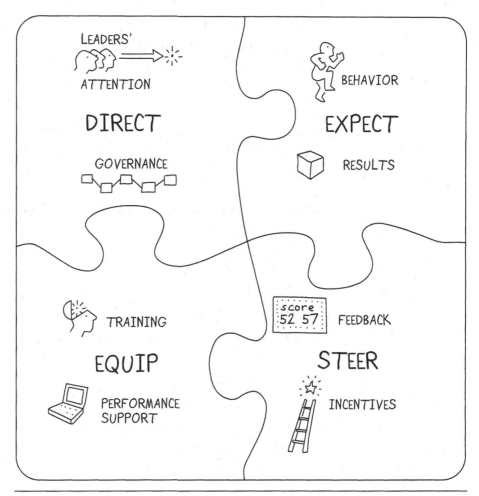

Lynn Kearny, CPT, Graphic Recorder

Chapter 2: How to Provide Direction. The goal of this chapter is to help managers and supervisors understand ways to provide direction despite any limitations in leadership. There are five tools in this chapter:

- Tool 2.1: How to Design a Governance Structure
- Tool 2.2: How to Develop and Use Cross-Functional Charts
- Tool 2.3: How to Develop Governing Principles, Protocols, and Ground Rules
- Tool 2.4: How to Develop Operating Guidelines and Procedures
- Tool 2.5: How to Develop and Use RASCI Charts

Role Two: Set Expectations

Chapter 3: How to Set Expectations. The goal of this chapter is to present ideas on how to identify and communicate expectations to employees. It includes defining deliverables, customers, and performance measures. There are three tools in this chapter:

- Tool 3.1: How to Identify Deliverables
- Tool 3.2: How to Evaluate Your Current Use of Measures
- Tool 3.3: How to Select Measures

Chapter 4: How to Identify Behaviors That Lead to Performance. The goal of this chapter is to present ideas on how to identify the behaviors that lead to performance and use them to communicate expectations. There are three tools in this chapter:

- Tool 4.1: How to Identify Desired Behaviors
- Tool 4.2: How to Develop Behavioral Interview Questions
- Tool 4.3: Job Aid for Describing Behaviors by Job Level and Level of Performance

  Part A—Senior Manager

  Part B—Mid-Level Manager

  Part C—First-Level Manager

  Part D—Supervisor

  Part E—Individual Contributor

Role Three: Equip People to Perform

Chapter 5: How to Use Orientations and Training Effectively. The goal of this chapter is to explain how to prepare people to do their jobs. It includes descriptions on how to orient and train people effectively. There are three tools in this chapter:

- Tool 5.1: How to Orient New Employees
- Tool 5.2: How to Get the Most from Training
- Tool 5.3: How to Make On-the-Job Training More Effective

Chapter 6: How to Use Job Aids to Support Performance. The goal of this chapter is to explain how to better equip people to do their jobs. It includes the appropriate use of job aids, standards, work rules, and procedures. There are two tools in this chapter:

- 6.1: How to Select and Use Job Aids
- 6.2: How to Identify and Use Standards, Work Rules, and Procedures

Role Four: Steer so People Stay on Course

Chapter 7: How to Make Giving Feedback Less Painful. The goal of this chapter is to present ideas on how to give people feedback in ways that are meaningful to them and less painful for the manager or supervisor. There are four tools in this chapter:

- Tool 7.1: How to Use Project Plans and Action Plans for Giving Feedback
- Tool 7.2: How to Use Meeting Guidelines to Give Feedback
- Tool 7.3: How to Obtain and Use Internal Customer Feedback
- Tool 7.4: Guidelines for Giving Feedback

Chapter 8: How to Recognize and Reward People. The goal of this chapter is to present ideas on how to shape people's performance through the use of incentives. There are three tools in this chapter:

- Tool 8.1: How to Identify Leading Indicators
- Tool 8.2: How to Identify and Select Incentives
- Tool 8.3: How to Align Recognition and Rewards

NOTES

1. The requirements for performance have been identified and validated by many people. One of those was Tom Gilbert, who presented his "Probe Model" as a framework for diagnosing why people do not perform as expected. His ideas were further developed in *Human Competence* (San Francisco, CA: Jossey-Bass, 1978).

2. Roger Kaufman suggests there are three levels of clients and beneficiaries of what any organization uses, does, produces, and delivers. He calls the primary client as society and community that he terms as Mega planning. When the primary client and beneficiary of what is used and done is the organization itself, it is termed macro planning, and when the target is individuals and small groups, that is "micro planning." Kaufman suggests that strategic thinking and planning is characterized by starting at the mega—societal level. Two of Kaufman's books that discuss the concept of worth are *Strategic Thinking: A Guide to Identifying and Solving Problems* (rev. ed.) (Arlington, VA/Washington, DC: American Society for Training & Development and the International Society for Performance Improvement, 1998) and *Mega Planning: Practical Tools for Organizational Success.* (Thousand Oaks, CA: Sage Publications, 2000).

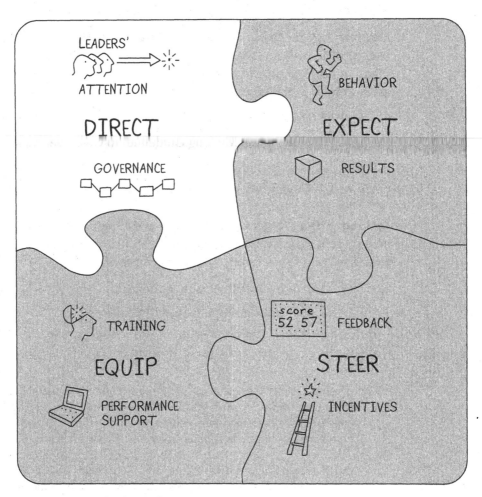

Figure 1.1. Leadership Roles

Lynn Kearny, CPT, Graphic Recorder

Chapter 1

How Leaders Set the Direction

What are we trying to do? Where are we headed?

*T*his chapter explains the role of leadership at all levels in the organization in providing direction. Leadership is like a beacon or navigational aid. People must know what the goal or destination is and they require signals over the course of their efforts to confirm that they are on track. No ship's captain would set sail without knowing the destination and having the ability to know whether or not he was on course. No airplane pilot would take off without knowing the destination and having the capability to validate whether or not the plane was on its prescribed flight path. Yet organizations repeatedly engage in activities and launch new initiatives, products, and technology without understanding or being in agreement on the goal or having the ability to stay on course.

People require three types of information to do their jobs effectively. The first type should come from top leadership, as it is about where the organization is headed, what the priorities are, and what the organization is doing in terms of investment to compete in the marketplace or fulfill its mission. The second type should come from human resources (HR) and the manager or supervisor, as it is about what is expected of individuals in terms of their roles, goals, and performance criteria. The third type comes from the training department and the manager or supervisor, as it is about what to do, how to do it, and why. Managers and supervisors have an important role in assuring that people receive all three types of information. This chapter focuses on how to use the information that comes from top management to make sure goals, objectives, deliverables, activities, and measures are aligned and understood by the people.

- A *goal* is an end state or condition toward which human effort is directed

- An *objective* is an interim or enabling state or condition that, when combined with other objectives, leads to a goal

- A *deliverable* is something that is produced to accomplish a goal or objective, a physical or mental object
- An *activity* is a combination of behaviors that contribute to creating a deliverable and achieving an objective
- A *measure* is an attribute that is used as the basis for judging productivity, proficiency, performance, and worth

PERFORMANCE IMPROVEMENT

From a performance improvement perspective, people deserve clear direction. They should have some understanding of what the organization is trying to accomplish and what role they play in making it happen. The first principle of performance is to focus on results — to not lose sight of the outcomes that are required to meet the organization's goals. Focus is about making sure goals, objectives, activities, deliverables, and measures are aligned and congruent. Once people know the goals, they should know what is expected of them. Once they know what is expected and the direction they are heading, they will require tools to help them perform the job. Finally, they should get cues or signals to help them stay on course.

COMMON MISSTEPS

Here are some common mistakes managers and supervisors make when it comes to assuring people receive the direction they deserve:

1. They assume that the members of top management are in agreement on the goals.
2. They assume that top management has thought through the implications of what they attend to and that they understand the effect of their shifting their attention or changing their message.
3. They assume that what they want to accomplish is understood and agreed to by the people who do the work and by those who depend on the work being done.
4. They create plans and set objectives without fully understanding the situation or thinking through the ramifications of their actions.
5. They assume there will be no negative side effects to how they go about work and that, if there are, they are in no position to reduce or eliminate them.
6. They fail to confirm that what they use, do, produce, and deliver is working toward the same goal.

7. They fail to exercise judgment when it comes to interpreting top management's behaviors or messages.

8. They assume that they are part of the solution and not part of the problem.

9. They fail to validate their assumptions.

LEADERSHIP

Leadership is not about standing up and saying, "I'm in charge!" but it does require leaders to behave in certain ways because it is their behaviors that reinforce or cue people in how to act. Leadership is what assures efforts are focused on the right goals, objectives, deliverables, and activities. It can and must occur at all levels so people are continually reminded of what is important, where the organization is headed, and what is required of them. Leadership can empower people if they understand where the organization is headed and they have confidence in their leaders. There are two sets of behaviors, in particular, that are especially important to providing direction.

1. *Focus on results* happens when leaders overtly state what the goal is, what the rules are for carrying out the work, what is and is not open for discussion or debate, what is expected of everyone, and what will be used as evidence of progress and success.

2. *Consistency of focus* is about leaders consistently sending the same messages about what the goal is and what is important. Mixed messages like "Avoid excess inventory but never run out of product" confuse people and distract them from the goal.

Focus on Results

Performance improvement begins by defining:

- The goals and results that you want to have happen or accomplish
- The deliverables or outputs required for you to achieve the results and what each group must produce to get the results
- The side effects of accomplishing the result, specifically the unforeseen implications you want to avoid, whether they are damaged relations or exhausted employees
- The sustainability of the effort, what it will take in energy and resources to continue to do the work time and time again (see Figure 1.2)

The terms *goals and objectives* and *goals and outcomes* are used interchangeably. However, there is usually an assumed hierarchy with goals having

**Figure 1.2. Ripple Effect
of Goals and Objectives**

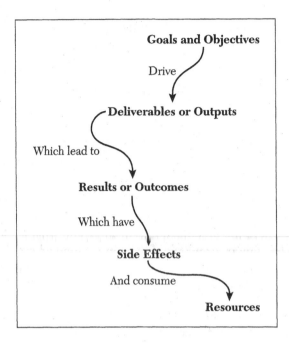

a broader meaning and objectives less so. Organizations set goals that are statements that describe what they want to achieve or become. Objectives are the interim milestones or deliverables that have to happen to accomplish the goals and they are usually more specific and more measurable.

People are hired to produce *deliverables* or *outputs* in the belief that the effort will lead to an *outcome,* such as more revenue, higher profits, strategic alliances, greater market penetration, and higher retention of customers. What they produce may be things, ideas, or information. However, what is produced or how it is produced usually has *side effects* that may or may not have been predicted. Side effects can be negative or positive. For example, sometimes the cost of the sale in *resources* exceeds the revenue gained and inventory cannot keep up with demand, damaging customer relations.

Sustainability is about the ability to continue to deliver in the long-term given the demand on your current resources. Tradeoffs usually have to be made to continue to sustain the results or reap the benefits over time. Some examples are having sufficient qualified people to sell, perform repairs, and service customers and having the dollars to purchase materials or invest in development.

Deliverables, in and of themselves, may not lead to desired results, and results may not have desirable side effects. The demands on resources to deliver or sustain the result may be so great as to limit the ability to take advantage of other opportunities or respond to new challenges.

GOALS, OBJECTIVES, AND OUTCOMES

Top management defines the goals for the organization. Other levels of management interpret the goals for their departments and then set goals or objectives specific for their groups. Then they develop plans or identify the activities required to accomplish the objectives and define the measures of success. Outcomes are the results that occur after having engaged in activities to meet the goals and objectives. An outcome is successful or not based on the measures that were used (see Figure 1.3).

Organization Level

- The organization's *goals* are profits, societal return on investment, market share, and market demand for products

- The organization's *outputs* or deliverables are all the goods and services it develops and delivers to the marketplace

- The *outcomes* are the results that occur from having produced the goods and services

- The *measures* are the criteria used to judge success or effectiveness, such as dollars, ratings, percentages, and so forth, both in the short-term and long-term

- The *side effects* of having achieved or not achieved the goals are the impact on its brand image and relationships with labor, customers, employees, distributors, third-party partners, investors, and regulatory agencies

- *Sustainability* is about having sufficient economic resources, access to materials and talent, and the production and distribution capacity to honor promises to customers, investors, employees, outside agencies, and partners in the future

Figure 1.3. Hierarchy of Goals and Objectives

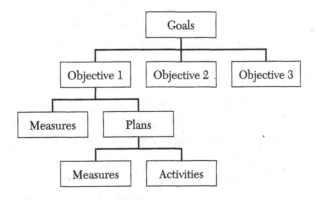

Here are some examples.

- A bank's goal is to service the financial needs of the community at a profit. A bank's products or outputs are loans, mortgages, investment advice, and savings and checking accounts. The outcome is number of services rendered and at what profit or loss. The impact or side effect is market share. Sustainability is about having qualified personnel to service customers and the resources to continue to offer competitive products.

- An airport's goal is to positively impact the economy of the local area. The airport's outputs are services to airlines and passengers that include landing strips, gates, facilities, parking, and concessions. The outcomes are revenues from gates and parking and jobs for concessionaires and other outsourced services. The side effect is economic impact on the community from taxes and spending by passengers, workers, and businesses supporting the airport and airlines. Sustainability depends on the airport's ability to maintain its facilities so it can attract airlines, passengers, and businesses.

Department or Division Level

- The *objectives* may include marketable products, profits, retention of customers and employees, cooperative labor-management relations, efficient distribution channels, and excellent customer service

- The *outputs* or deliverables required to achieve the objectives might include the development of products, marketing strategies, agreements, and policies required to manufacture, promote, sell, distribute, and provide after-market support to the marketplace

- The *outcome* is the results that were achieved or what actually happened from having delivered the products or services

- The *side effects* may be higher than anticipated customer loyalty, unexpected innovation by employees, higher yields in investments, and the ability to leverage relationships with distributors to service new markets or the opposite

- The *measures* might include the number of products that reached market, the degree of market penetration, the number of customers retained, and the level of employee and customer satisfaction

- *Sustainability* is having the bench strength in facilities, equipment, systems, people, and processes to withstand new competition, changing requirements, increased regulation, and other market pressures

Here are some examples.

- The objectives of the bank's loan department include profitable loans. The outputs of the bank's loan department are its lending instruments, such as mortgages, home equity loans, and college loans. The outcomes are the earnings from those loans. The side effect might be losses from bad loans or an increased number of customers making use of other bank services because of their loan experience. Sustainability is about the loan officers' ability to develop and maintain relationships with local businesses and residents in the community and continue to offer cost-competitive, yet profitable, products.

- The objectives of the airport maintenance department are good relations with airlines and concessionaires and passengers because of functioning jetways, escalators, elevators, and so forth. The outputs are the repair and maintenance of facilities, such as jetways, people movers, bathrooms, escalators, and utilities to restaurants, concessions, and other retail businesses. The outcome is the level of satisfaction airlines, concessions, and passengers have with the airport. The side effects are avoided complaints and lawsuits due to malfunctioning equipment, power outages, or poorly maintained bathrooms. The sustainability is about the airport having the financial ability to retain qualified people to maintain the facilities and buy quality equipment.

Work Unit, Team, and Individual Levels

- The *objectives* might include meeting production quotas, satisfying internal and external customers, and controlling costs, as well as setting up capable distribution channels

- The *outputs* may be the development and delivery of sub-assemblies, prototypes, marketing materials, training, documentation, and other resources required to build, market, and deliver products to customers, provide customer service, operate systems, and assure that employees are capable

- The *outcomes* are the actual results achieved from having created the outputs

- The *side effects* could be trust, cooperation, shorter cycle times, safer performance, lower reject rates, and higher productivity or they might be the ability to rapidly deploy staff to new production lines or field offices in response to unanticipated demand or interrupted distribution capability

- The *measures* might include the volume and cost of production, the number of distribution channels set up, and at what cost

- *Sustainability* depends on the ability to handle increased capacity and changing requirements and on the employees having the energy and willingness to continue to innovate and produce at the same level of intensity over time (If you do not have the right people you cannot sustain performance)

Here are some examples.

- At the bank a loan officer's objective may be to lend a minimum dollar amount. The outputs are the number and dollar value of loans approved. The outcome is the profit generated from the loans, any losses that may occur, and accurate and cost-efficient transactions. The side effects are satisfied customers and the number of customers purchasing other bank services. The sustainability depends on the loan officer's continued interest in serving customers and staying current in banking regulations and on the bank's ability to retain qualified loan officers and friendly tellers.

- The objective of the airport maintenance department is no loss of revenue or life because of accidents on slippery runways or roads. The outputs of the groundskeeping department are clean, cleared runways and access roads and attractive landscaping. The outcome is the amount of revenue lost or accidents that occurred due to poorly maintained runways and access roads. The side effect is compliments by passengers, the airlines' confidence in the airport, and community pride in the attractiveness of the area. Sustainability depends on the airport continuing to allocate resources for the maintenance of the grounds.

Here is a set of guidelines to help your work group understand their role in the organization.

TOOL 1.1: HOW TO IDENTIFY GOALS AND OBJECTIVES

Purpose

This guideline is designed to help your work unit gain an understanding of what their goals and objectives are. It can help you determine whether your understanding of your deliverables is the same as what others in the organization think.

How

You can start the process; however, you may want to ask someone from training or HR to assist.

A. Begin with the department or division your group is part of.
  1. What are the goals of the department or division?
  2. What does the department or division as a whole produce? What are its deliverables?
  3. What are the outcomes it wants to achieve?
  4. What are the side effects it hopes to avoid? Remember to consider factors like relationships, image, cost overruns, and a drain on resources.
  5. What will it take to sustain the level of performance it wants? Consider things like there is no change in top management, breakthroughs in technology happen at a pace the organization can support, or that promises to customers about new products or services are met.
  6. What attributes, criteria, or factors will the department or division use to measure its success?
B. Now ask the same six questions of your particular work unit or group.
C. Share your answers with your peers and manager to identify any differences or things you did not think of.
D. If there is any discrepancy or disagreement over what they believe you do and what the results should be, work with them to resolve the discrepancy.
E. Use what you learn to develop goals and objectives for your group and identify the criteria to judge what you do.

Hint: When you go through the exercise, think about how much has stayed the same over the last year or so, how much has changed, and to what degree the emphasis has changed. Pay attention to any trends, as this insight will help you when setting priorities for your group.

Here is an example of how one organization works to align its goals, objectives, and deliverables to achieve the desired results.

DULLES AIRPORT

Background
The airport authority has the dual role of managing a major metropolitan airport and supporting the economic stability of the community through its employment and contracting practices. It has approximately 1,200 full-time employees, most of whom work for airport operations, engineering, and maintenance. The authority also provides jobs for another 26,000 people at the airport, including contractors involved in the construction of new runways,

parking garages, and concourses; those who work for the concessions (restaurants and retail stores); and those who do housekeeping and work in the parking garage.

The Goals and Objectives

Two years ago the airport implemented a new strategic planning process based on a modified balanced-scorecard.[1] The planning process was designed to help departments link their objectives and performance measures to one or more of the airport's goals—safety and security, customer and partner satisfaction, efficient operations, and growth and development. At the same time it introduced a performance management system (PMP). The objectives of the strategic planning process and PMP are to drive decision making down in the organization, force greater collaboration across departments, and link rewards to performance instead of being an entitlement. The goal is a cost-efficient airport that is attractive to airlines and supports the local economy.

The Objective

The airport manager at Dulles has as one of his objectives the identification and improvement of a major process. He chose maintenance because the cost of maintenance had steadily increased over the years, partially due to the increase in the number of facilities to be maintained and partly due to the aging of facilities. The current computer maintenance system could not measure productivity, accurately identify costs, track material usage, manage inventory, or assure efficient scheduling of personnel. The increasing demands on maintenance raised questions about how to best manage this function.

The airport manager commissioned a study of his maintenance operations and current computer system. The study showed that maintenance was a reactive rather than a planned process and that the current system could not provide the information required to manage the function effectively. A new system presented an opportunity to improve results and change the way maintenance was managed. At the same time, there was the challenge of how to continue providing maintenance services using the old system during the time of transition to a new computer system.

The Deliverable and Expected Result

A cross-functional planning team was appointed to decide how to implement the new system. The team had representatives from all the departments in maintenance—labor, materials, construction, electrical, mechanical, plumbing, and the work order desk. The team's deliverable was a plan on how to implement the new maintenance management process. The expected results were (1) a workable process for managing and resourcing all phases of the implementation effort while servicing current needs, (2) a process that would lead to a fundamental shift in how maintenance was managed that was collaborative, responsive to customers, and cost-efficient, and (3) a clarification of roles and responsibilities between maintenance, operations, and customers.

The airport manager was focused on results and worked to align his PMP to support his goals. What follows is another example; however, this company lost sight of what it wanted to accomplish.

PLASTICS

Background

Corp USA is a manufacturer of plastic building materials. It sold its products through numerous independent distributors. Two years ago management decided to buy one of its largest distributors, Premier. A year later it bought the second-largest distributor, a family-owned business, Sons. Before they were purchased, Premier and Sons had from 80 to 90 percent of the market share of the distribution of plastic building products.

The Goal

Corp USA's goal was to be the largest manufacturer and distributor of plastic building materials to the construction industry.

The Decisions/Actions

Brand Name: As soon as Corp USA acquired Premier, and later Sons, it created a new division called Plastics Distributors. *Plastics* ceased using the names Premier and Sons almost immediately after it acquired them.

Pricing Policies: Next, Plastics increased the prices charged by Premier and Son. The reason for the increase was Corp USA's policy that required every division to price its products with the same fixed percentage margin, a much higher margin than what Premier or Sons had used in the past. Sales staff were not allowed to consider the condition of the local market in terms of competition or the size of the order when pricing products. The higher prices went into effect immediately.

Staffing: To reduce costs, Plastics fired the more senior experienced outside and inside sales staff. While they drew more commissions than the less experienced salespeople, these were the people who had established relationships with customers. They had technical expertise and knew their customers' business issues. Many operated on a first-name basis with customers. The people who remained had less seniority, and therefore were paid less, but they also lacked the technical expertise to discuss the product's application with the customer.

The Results and Aftereffects

Loss of Business: Within a year, Plastics had lost over 50 percent of the business it acquired with the purchase of Premier and Sons. The higher prices due to the higher fixed margins angered the larger customers, who were use to price considerations when they placed large orders.

Loss of Brand Image: The change in name angered many customers, who wanted to know who they were suddenly dealing with and why the person they were used to dealing with was not there.

Loss of Buying Power: The loss of business also reduced Plastics' buying power with manufacturers. It no longer had the clout that comes with being a big volume buyer.

Growth of Competition: The experienced people who had been laid off joined smaller distributors who were merging. The salespeople leveraged their relationships with old customers and their knowledge of the customers' business to win prize accounts. These smaller yet growing distributors were willing to accept lower margins to get the business. They sold on volume and this increased their buying power with the manufacturers.

What Happened

Plastics management had manufacturing backgrounds and no experience in distribution. They did not understand the nature of the business. Had they done some investigation they would have learned:

- The distribution of building plastics is a low-margin business
- Selling building plastics requires technical expertise in how acrylics are made and used by customers
- Sales depend on knowing your customers' businesses and building a good relationship with each customer
- Customers who buy in large volume expect price considerations, perhaps in the form of lower margins, a reduction in some or all shipping costs, or not charging extra for multiple shipments or shipments to multiple locations

The New Challenge

Plastics Distributors is now trying to get back the business it lost. It has the best inventory and inventory management system in the industry. It offers better service than the competition, but its prices are not competitive. The new sales reps know the market potential, but the big customers do not trust them or Plastics because of the name change, higher prices, and firing of people who had learned their business.

Management at Plastics did not do a sufficient analysis of the situation to understand the distribution business and what customers expected; therefore, it was not able to provide the direction required to stay competitive.

MESSAGES AND DIRECTION

We are in the business of making money for stockholders! [The words that were deleted were "building safe airplanes."]

Our overarching principles are value, uninterrupted supply. [The words that were deleted were "safe" and "family friendly."]

Top management communicates what is important by:

* What is and is not mentioned publicly, during briefings, meetings, and announcements
* Who is left out, not invited, or not given time to speak at meetings
* The order in which topics are addressed
* The amount of time, dollars, and talent committed to a topic

People assign meaning based on where management focuses its attention. Says Ed Schein:

"What leaders consistently pay attention to communicates most clearly what their own priorities, goals, and assumptions are. If they pay attention to too many things or if their pattern of attention is inconsistent, subordinates will use other signals or their own experience to decide what is really important, leading to a much more diverse set of assumptions and many more subcultures."[2]

To find out what management and others think is important, examine:

* What is and is not on the agenda of formal meetings
* How much time is allotted to different topics and the sequence of the topics
* Who is and is not included in formal and informal communications
* Who is and is not included in meetings
* Who is and is not afforded time to speak

CONSISTENCY

Top management begins the process of providing direction when it establishes the goals for the year. Next, middle management provides direction for first-line managers and supervisors by setting department goals based on its interpretation of top management's messages and behavior. Finally, first-line managers and supervisors provide direction for their work units based on their interpretation of their management's behavior and messages. This trickle-down process only works when the goals that are communicated are congruent with what management pays attention to and with what gets measured, and if what gets measured supports the intended results.

Therefore, leaders provide direction in what they attend to and what they measure, not necessarily by what they say are the goals. However, what gets their attention and is measured should be consistent with what they said were the goals. Unfortunately, this does not always happen. Worse, compensation and bonus plans do not always support what the company says it wants its people to accomplish. As a result, some companies are now basing a portion of managers' bonuses on the performance of the work unit over more than one year and have even extended the performance period for twenty-four to thirty-six months. This sends an especially strong message if the manager is on a rotational assignment, makes some change, or implements an initiative and then goes on to the next assignment, never to experience the impact of his or her decisions.

The Burial of Past Initiatives

A part of being consistent is taking the time to formally end or bring closure to previous initiatives. Organizations repeatedly launch initiatives in support of the goals; however, they rarely show how the new programs support or build on ones introduced earlier. The familiar scenario is that managers are herded into a one-day or two-day training session about the new initiative and leave with a three-ring binder. Six months later the scenario is repeated. No one talks about how long it takes to reap the benefits of the first initiative. Research shows it takes up to six years to fully implement and reap the benefits of a change, a new process, or a new organizational structure.[3] The constant launch of new initiatives can cause confusion and lead to cynicism. Top management should either formally bring to close past initiatives or be explicit about how new ones are building on the past. When this does not happen, you have some choices to make. For example, you can try to find the relationship between the old and new and take the responsibility for building bridges for your people. You can help your manager do it for you by asking if and when you can drop your efforts to implement previous program recommendations. You can renegotiate your performance goals for the year, making explicit what you will no longer be doing, and you can begin to track the cost implications of half-implemented ideas. The important thing to remember is that doing nothing and remaining silent sends a message and that may be counter to what you want your people to believe and act on. Here is a set of guidelines to help you be aware of top management's messages and topic of attention.

TOOL 1.2: HOW TO IDENTIFY WHAT IS IMPORTANT

Purpose

The intent of this set of guidelines is to make you more aware of how top management communicates its expectations by what captures its attention.

How

With your boss or peers:

   A. Find out:
   1. What is and is not on top management's agenda of formal meetings.
   2. How much time is allotted to different topics and the sequence of the topics.
   3. Who is and is not included in formal and informal communications.
   4. Who is and is not included in meetings.
   5. Who is and is not afforded time to speak during formal meetings.

   B. If you are unable to answer the questions above, identify people with whom you need to develop a better relationship so that you are in a position to more accurately interpret top management's behaviors and messages.

   C. Go back to the first of the fiscal year and locate the goals for the year.
   1. Have any of them changed?
   2. How do you know? On what behaviors or messages are you basing your conclusions?
   3. Compare your answers to the above questions to what top management said were the goals of the organization.
   4. How might you reconcile the new silence about what was important with the new noise about what is important?

   D. Think about your own messages over the past year.
   1. Have they changed?
   2. Do you regularly discuss or ask people to report on their progress related to what you said were the goals, as this is how you demonstrate consistency?
   3. Do you try to show the relationship between old messages and new ones?

Hint: Changing direction is not a bad thing to do, when the change is warranted. However, you should be aware of when you change your message and the implication on others' behavior. Remember that what is not said communicates as much if not more than what is said.

OFF THE CUFF

Statements are made in meetings and on the fly. Some of those statements are top management "thinking out loud" and others are merely wish lists but are couched like rules or goals. The onus is on you to interpret what you heard or have been told, decide how much latitude you really have, and figure out how to reframe the message in a way that better reflects the intent. Do you honor the spirit of the statement or its literal meaning? Sometimes honoring the literal statement can be malicious obedience, especially if you know that is not in the best interest of the organization. Here is an example.

OVERTIME

Steve managed a research facility. One day his boss returned from an all-managers meeting and his first words were, "Well, there's no more overtime!" It seems top management's attention had changed to cost containment and their statements made it sound like cutting out overtime was a goal rather than one possible solution. Steve, however, knew that overtime in some circumstances was less costly than forcing work to be completed within a shift. Steve managed highly skilled tradesmen who were responsible for the maintenance of very sophisticated equipment that simulated different atmospheric conditions that scientists required for their experiments. The equipment operated around the clock, seven days a week. If the equipment failed or did not perform to standard, it affected the results of experiments and the schedules of hundreds of people and put very expensive materials at risk. Equipment does not always break at convenient times. Steve could interpret the message "no overtime" as a rule or a goal instead of as a proposed solution to a larger goal, probably related to reducing costs. If he interpreted it as a rule, the next time the equipment required service and could not be completely repaired during that shift, he would tell the tradesman to stop and come back the next day to complete the work. It could mean scientists would stand idle because they could not continue to work.

Steve's response to his boss was, "Why don't we talk now, because at the end of the year either you're going to be disappointed with my performance or I'm going to be disappointed with my review!" Steve restated top management's message as wanting to reduce costs and as suggesting that overtime may be one way to accomplish it. He went on to suggest some guidelines for when overtime might be appropriate and how his boss might justify it. He also suggested that he and his peers work together to find other ways to reduce costs.

How much latitude you have to reinterpret or reframe top management's messages depends on:

- The amount of time you have been with the organization, as seniority should have given you an opportunity to demonstrate that your actions are in the best interest of the company and build relationships with people who have access to top management. In Steve's case he had continuously demonstrated that he was a good corporate soldier and had implemented many cost savings in his career.

- Whether or not you have the support of your peers. There is strength in numbers. Steve isn't the only manager whose crew's schedule can affect the work of highly paid scientists and engineers.

- The amount of access you have to top management or the people who influence them so that you can informally explain your position. It is important to build relationships with people at all levels in the organization. You never know when you will need a friend.

- Your level of knowledge, self-confidence, or belief in what you want to do. Doubt can lead to hesitancy. Self-confidence comes from doing your homework, understanding your work unit's role in the organization, and knowing how your work impacts others.

You don't have to have all of these factors, but the more you do have the stronger your position to interpret your company's direction in ways that make sense for your operation. Here is a set of guidelines to help you evaluate the feasibility of your challenging mixed messages effectively.

TOOL 1.3: HOW TO CHALLENGE MIXED MESSAGES

Purpose

To assess your readiness to challenge mixed or unclear messages.

How

Alone or with trusted colleagues meet to discuss the following points. The goal is to assess your readiness to challenge or reinterpret the direction you are given because you want to support the organization's goals.

A. Think back on those times when you experienced disconnects between what was supposedly the "goal" and what the leadership was paying attention to.

1. What did you do that worked to resolve this disconnect?

2. What might you have done differently?

B. If vague or mixed messages are typical where you work, alone or preferably with your peers:

1. Identify what you think the goal or message should be.

2. Begin (if you haven't done so already) to document the effect of the vague or mixed messages, such as the number of false starts, time spent doing rework, or people engaged in activities that are counterproductive.

3. Come up with suggestions about how you might approach your manager with recommendations on how to clarify the message or connect it to what you think is important.

C. Ask yourself who benefits from mixed messages. Confusion can be a distraction whether it is from inadequate leadership or from poorly designed processes.

D. Begin to build a plan to increase your own credibility and ability to challenge mixed messages and assure your people are working on the right goals.

1. Identify people in the organization who are either decision makers or in a position to influence others' decisions. They might include key internal customers, your boss's peers, or important suppliers.

2. Think about how you might establish a relationship with them so that you can present your ideas when it is appropriate. One way is to ask to meet with them to better understand their expectations of your group and how your work affects them. Then use the time to better understand their issues, processes, and expectations. Later, they may be willing to hear your issues as well; however, start by showing your interest in them before you ask them to take up your cause.

3. Learn to be a champion of your group's efforts. Craft and send messages to your boss and key internal customers about your group's successes and efforts to improve efficiency and customer satisfaction. You want a reputation as someone who is focused on results that contribute to the success of the organization.

4. Ask yourself how much initiative you are willing to take to help your manager provide consistent direction.

Hint: Consistent direction helps people stay focused on results. You cannot control what top management does, but you can control your own messages.

People shape their behavior based on what they see management attending to and by what is counted. Top management's job is to assure that what they pay attention to and measure gives them an accurate understanding of how well the organization is doing. Your job is to transform what the organization measures to criteria that make sense for your work unit and can be tracked. Human performance depends on the goals and measures being aligned; otherwise there is confusion and the misdirection of resources. Here is an example of misaligned goals and measures.

PORTLAND CEMENT

A plant can produce as much as 3.5 million tons of portland cement a year. The kilns used to make the product are long cylindrical furnaces rotating along their axis. These kilns can be as long as 760 feet with diameters large enough for a locomotive to pass through. Kiln operation is the key to production. The kiln heats powdered limestone, shale, and other materials to temperatures approaching one fourth the temperature of the surface of the sun. The intense heat partially melts the material and transforms the powdered rock blend into portland cement clinker.

Cement plants operate twenty-four hours, seven days a week with operation targeted for more than 330 days each year. The remaining days are used for maintenance and to repair the kiln system. It takes from two to three days for these mammoth furnaces to cool down sufficiently for an inspector to enter and check for damage. Crews then do the required repairs for the coming year.

Top management says it wants plant managers to protect the assets of the plant and operate safely while meeting the production quota. However, the only thing that gets measured is amount of cement produced, and the plant manager's bonus goes up when he exceeds the goal. The amount of cement a plant can produce is dictated by the number of days the kiln is in operation over the course of the year. Plants can exceed the production quota if the kiln operators are encouraged to "run hot" and "run fast." The damage from running hot and fast may not become evident for days or even weeks, but it does occur. Running at full capacity continuously does not increase profits or decrease maintenance. Some costs are more immediate, such as increased maintenance costs or fines for air pollution. Others costs are non-economic, such as loss of community good will due to the pollution of the air and ground water. Eventually all costs are borne by the plant due to breakdowns and lost production. A plant could even be put out of commission for weeks or months for repairs.

Because top management only attended to the amount produced annually, rather than to what was produced over a series of years, it contributed to a cyclical operation—high production year followed by a low production year—rather than optimal production over many years. The plant manager in turn continued the cycle of sub-optimizing production by rewarding kiln operators on the quantity of production for their shift rather than the yield of all three shifts. Operators who exceeded the shift goal were labeled heroes. Any operator can exceed set production goals for a short period of time if he either runs the kiln hot or accelerates the flow of materials through the system. However, subsequent operators have to reduce production to prevent damage to the system caused by overheating, which harms the refractory lining of the furnace. This can and does lead to cyclical operation, which yields less production in the long run than if each shift had just held to the set shift production objectives. Top management and the plant manager's behaviors ultimately undermined the long-term performance of the plant and the organization as a whole.

If you were the shift manager or supervisor at the cement plant, what could you do to help break the cycle? One thing you might do is to stop competing with the other shift managers and supervisors. In many organizations the expression "management team" or "supervisory team" is an oxymoron. The words "manager" or "supervisor" and "team" in the same sentence do not make sense because the organization fosters internal competition in how it measures performance and compensates people. However, you and your manager can set measures that foster trust and collaboration instead of competition among the managers and supervisors. You will have to meet with your peers and come to some agreement about how you will measure your performance and the productivity of your people. Another way to break the cycle is to evaluate people on more than just one factor, such as:

- Meeting the production goal within some range. For the cement plant this might be staying within the recommended yield ± some percent (tonnage or other measure), AND

- Meeting cost goals within some range. For the cement plant this might be fuel costs, sporadic outages, and pollution violations, AND

- Not impacting the next shift or the department that receives your group's work negatively. In the case of the cement plant this might be NOT making the next shift run slower or cooler because of your shift running fast or hot, AND

- Not violating any safety regulations. In the case of the cement plant this would be not producing emissions that exceed the air pollution standards.

You might even suggest that part of your own, your peers,' and your people's bonus be based on the plant's overall production goal for the year and it meeting some public commitment for safety. Here's another example.

JERRY THE MECHANIC

Jerry is a master mechanic who supervises a crew that maintains a fleet of trucks. Early in his career he noticed who got ahead in the company and who did not. He observed that some managers operated on the lean or "squeeze out all you can" model of management. These managers became company heroes because they delivered faster, cut costs, and exceeded production quota. They were rapidly promoted, only to inflict damage somewhere else. What they really did was shift costs to the future or to others because they would not invest in maintenance, process improvement, or any activity that takes resources away from producing for the moment.

What happens in situations like Jerry's is that managers exceed the capacity of their systems (both human and mechanical) and, as a result, the managers who follow them risk being called "under-performers" because their costs are high due to breakdowns, repairs, replacements, or turnover. Again, the question is what you should do in a situation like Jerry's. You could do nothing. However, if you were the one inheriting poorly maintained equipment and exhausted people, you might not like that choice. In terms of performance improvement, "doing nothing" is unacceptable because it fails to consider the aftereffects of the choice. Another choice is to meet with your manager and suggest adding goals such as meeting equipment maintenance specifications within some range. You might also negotiate a different set of measures with your boss, ones that reflect the real capacity of your equipment and people and do not shift costs to the future. Here is another example.

LEGAL DEPARTMENT'S EXPECTATIONS

Linda is a corporate attorney. The lawyers in her department are assigned to geographic regions. Linda handles the legal needs of the company's interests in Eastern Europe. The legal department has a rule that the lawyers may not exceed budget for specific legal line items. For example, Linda is required to specify how much she expects to spend on litigation, patents, regulatory work, outside council to handle acquisitions or the sale of facilities, and general council. She even has to specify which legal firms she will use and what the budget will be. By comparison, other companies' legal departments set up a contingency fund for unexpected legal costs that is available to the whole department and can be used for whatever unforeseen costs occur. If Linda and the other lawyers exceed their budgeted estimates, they lose their bonuses; however, if they are under budget, the excess funds are classified as operating profit. Their annual bonus is based on staying within the line item budget and on how much they contribute to the operating profit.

What gets measured has led to some interesting behavior that is not in the best interest of the company. For example, the lawyers inflate their budgets so they are less likely to exceed them. This inflation creates a false profit. If the lawyers think they will exceed their budget, they ask the business unit manager to pay the legal fees, thus shifting the costs to the client. Asking the client to pay makes it difficult to get an accurate understanding of the cost for legal ser vices. The company ends up not knowing what it spends for legal services.

Unfortunately, inflated budgets are a common practice that distorts real costs and supports bad decisions. What might you do to assure that the rules and performance measures support top management having a clear picture of what its costs are? Just as with the previous examples, you might confirm that top management wants an accurate view of what is happening in the organization. You might meet with other lawyers to gather some data, collect examples, document the problem, and present recommendations that encourage cost containment and discourage inflated budgets. You could suggest that, instead of meeting budget, a range be established, such as actual costs should fall somewhere between a target number plus and minus so many thousands of dollars. Whatever measures you come up with should encourage a more accurate accounting of expenditures and a realistic picture of performance.

TIPS

Here are some suggestions to help you stay focused.

1. Do your homework. Figure out whether the rules, what gets counted, and what top management attends to encourages or discourages the type of behaviors and results you want to see.

2. Accept the fact that there are constraints, but don't assume you have to accept them, at least long-term. Change comes from believing in the future.

3. Pretend you are the person whose pay and potential for promotion will be judged if you meet the numbers. What will you do to make the numbers

support your personal goals? Will this in any way undermine the organization meeting its goal?

4. Develop relationships with the people who are vested in keeping things the same and those who want to see changes. You want both as your allies.

5. Be skeptical, not cynical.

6. Continually ask questions to go to the assumptive base behind decisions. You want to know whether they are based on facts, hope, or hearsay.

7. Help your manager bring closure to past programs or show how they relate to new ones.

SUMMARY

The process in most organizations is for top management to communicate what it sees as the goals for the coming year and how they will be measured. It is especially important that the stated measures be congruent, be appropriate for the different business units, and support the organization's short-term and long-term goals. People notice when the information, behaviors, and results that leaders attend to are not consistent with their original message. At a minimum, leaders should repeatedly send the messages that reinforce the same goal, priorities, and course of action. If the priorities change, leaders should acknowledge that the focus has changed. Leaders are seen as consistent when they reward behaviors and results that are congruent with what they said were the goals, keep the same issues on their agenda, and regularly ask about the status of work they had previously said was important. Consistency and congruency are what distinguish leadership from management.

It is your job to interpret and translate the policy, goals, and measures so they are meaningful to the work group. You also have the job of giving top management feedback on the utility of their information. Therefore, make sure that what you pay attention to supports the organization's goals and professed values. At the same time, you must help your boss stay focused on what makes sense over time. Therefore, in collaboration with co-workers, staff, and your internal customers:

- Define the deliverable at whatever level is appropriate for you
- Specify what the expected and assumed outcome is
- Specify what aftereffects you want to avoid or have happen
- Identify the energy and resources that will be required to sustain the outcomes beyond the immediate period of time in question

The remainder of this book addresses specific things you can do to assure that your group performs at the level you expect.

WHERE TO LEARN MORE

Here are some useful books to learn more about leading and providing direction.

Byrd, R. E., *Guide to Personal Risk Taking* (New York, AMACOM, 1974). The book may be old, but it is not out-of-date. The book (paperback and about 200 pages) is written specifically for mid-level managers and is full of little assessments and ideas. You can buy it on www.Amazon.com or at www.addall.com.

Caroselli, M. *The Language of Leadership* (Amherst, MA: HRD Press, 1990). An easy and informative read with a linguist's observations about how leaders communicate. About 240 pages.

Daniels, W. R. *Breakthrough Performance: Managing for Speed and Flexibility* (Mill Valley, CA: ACT Publishing, 1995). Check out Chapter 1 titled "Who Cares? Your Role Set," as it is about choosing to manage and Chapter 4, as it is about setting expectations.

Fairhurst, G., and Sarr, R. *The Art of Framing: Managing the Language of Leadership* (San Francisco, CA: Jossey-Bass, 1996). This is a very interesting book (about 200 pages) on how managers do and should frame their messages to influence the behaviors and attitudes of other people.

Kaufman, R. *Strategic Thinking: A Guide to Identifying and Solving Problems* (rev. ed.) (Arlington, VA/Washington, DC: American Society for Training & Development and the International Society for Performance Improvement, 1998). Also published in Spanish: *El Pensamiento Estrategico: Una Guia Para Identificary Resolver los Problemas* (Madrid: Editorial Centros de Estudios Ramon Areces, S.A.).

Kaufman, R., Oakley-Browne, H., Watkins, R., and Leigh, D. *Strategic Planning for Success: Aligning People, Performance, and Payoffs* (San Francisco, CA: Jossey-Bass, 2003). The book comes with a CD-ROM full of tools.

Kriegel, R., and Brandt, D. *Sacred Cows Make the Best Burgers* (New York: Time Warner, 1996). A great paperback (approximately 250 pages) that is full of ideas. Pay particular attention to the authors' list of trust builders and trust busters.

Larkin, T. J., and Larkin, S. *Communicating Change: Winning Employee Support for a New Business Goal* (New York: McGraw-Hill, 1994). This book describes how managers can better explain why a new goal is necessary.

Mourier, P., and Smith, M. *Conquering Organizational Change: How to Succeed Where Most Companies Fail* (Atlanta, GA: CEP Press, 2001). This is a well-researched paperback of about 200 pages that is well worth your time.

NOTES

1. The Balanced Scorecard is a reference to Robert S. Kaplan and David P. Norton's excellent book *The Balanced Scorecard* published by Harvard Business Review Press, Boston, MA, 1996.

2. Schein, E. *Organizational Culture and Leadership* (2nd ed.) (San Francisco, CA: Jossey-Bass, 1992). This is an excellent book. Pay particular attention to pages 12 (his definition of culture), 17 (his levels of culture), 19 (how people derive a shared basis of reality), 231 (culture-embedding mechanisms), 281 (assumptions about

the nature of information), 282 (assumptions about people and learning), 286 (assumptions about organization and management), and 290 (assumptions about senior management). The quote appears on page 237.

3. Mary Gelinas and Roger James have done extensive research on why initiatives to improve organizational performance fail. Their program, *Collaborative Change: Improving Organizational Performance* (San Francisco, CA: Jossey-Bass, 1998), comes with a complete set of guidelines on how to implement and institutionalize change so you reap the benefits.

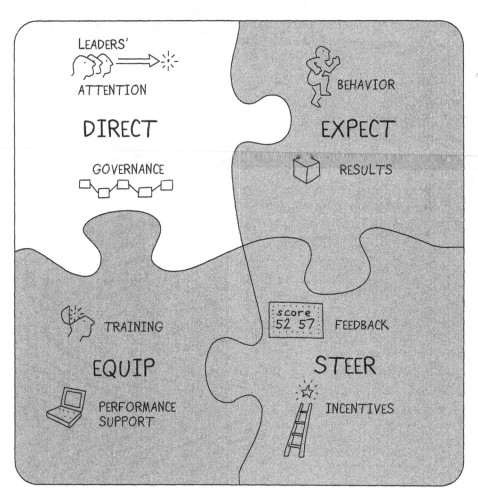

Figure 2.1. Leadership Roles

Lynn Kearny, CPT, Graphic Recorder

Chapter 2

How to Provide Direction

So how do things get done around here?

*T*his chapter continues with the importance of direction and explains ways to assure that you and others receive what you require to proceed when leadership by itself is inadequate, inefficient, vague, inconsistent, or overburdened. Martin Smith in his research[1] determined that the factors that correlated with failure were ineffective, missing, or conflicting leadership; vague goals; lack of a plan; and no one seemingly in charge.

Personnel at all levels want to know where they stand in relation to the organization's goals. The premise is that, without clear and consistent direction, organizations, departments, work groups, teams, and individuals can lose sight of where they are going. Effective leadership prevents groups from straying or shifting their focus to activities less likely to contribute to the outcomes required for success. However, relying on leadership by itself is insufficient. People also require protocols and governance structures that assure that decisions and approvals are made.

PERFORMANCE IMPROVEMENT

One of the strengths of performance improvement is the recognition that a variety of solutions can be used to assure people have what they require to be effective. Among those solutions are the use of systems and structures. This chapter explains how to set up governance structures and protocols to supplement the desired leadership behaviors.

In addition to being focused on results, there are two other behaviors people expect of their leaders:

1. *Legitimacy*—a set of behaviors that publicly signal that the organization endorses or approves certain roles and endeavors. The behaviors include

35

making public announcements that a goal, project, group, governance structure, or protocol has management's endorsement and support. Ideally, the messages are delivered in person.

2. *Expediency*—the behaviors that facilitate the work and efforts of others. Timeliness is the most important. Managers have to live up to their commitment to review work and render decisions in a timely fashion so as not to delay or obstruct the work of others. They should review recommendations, make decisions, and communicate their concerns as quickly as possible. Delays can communicate indecisiveness and result in people creating ways to circumvent the agreed-on way to do business.

Unfortunately, you cannot always get senior management to legitimize efforts or review and approve work in a timely fashion. However, there are some other things you can do to work around these deficiencies. People can still receive the direction they require if you have:

- A formal governance structure that defines how and by whom decisions are made that affect more than one function or department

- Public endorsement by senior management of the legitimacy of the governance structure

- Agreement on how messages will be communicated formally and informally and by whom

- Regular report-outs to the appropriate people in the organization on key decisions and what's been accomplished to date

- Operational protocols to guide decisions, collaboration, and coordination across divisions and work groups

- Formal recognition of everyone's contribution along the way, not just annually or when a major milestone is met

COMMON MISSTEPS

Here are some of the more common mistakes managers and supervisors make:

1. They fail to keep major initiatives designed to support the mission on the leader's agenda for more than a few months. Important work deserves attention.

2. They think an announcement at the beginning of a year or the launch of a new initiative or a memo announcing the goals for the year is sufficient to keep people on track.

3. They fail to recognize that people require a process or a method to debate and explore new ideas without censorship.

4. They discount people's need for guidelines on how to communicate with other departments and people in higher positions in the organization and ask for their support.

GOVERNANCE

Governance is about (1) how decisions are made related to priorities and the deployment of resources; (2) how and by whom those decisions are communicated to the rest of the organization; and (3) how decisions are to be implemented. Traditionally, organizations relied on the formal chain of command to define responsibilities, reporting relationships, and accountability and to handle the communication. Information goes up the chain and decisions and information come back down. This works when initiatives are contained within departments. However, many initiatives involve work processes that rarely fall within the boundaries of one department. Even how regular work is executed affects other departments and customers. Therefore, following the formal chain of command may be inefficient or produce undesired side effects. Instead, organizations require new governance structures to assure deliberation and cross-functional coordination of resources and communication. The new structure may be temporary or evolve into a more permanent yet collaborative way of doing business.

A governance structure defines roles, relationships, and reporting requirements, not unlike an organizational chart that shows how work is divvied up across divisions and departments. Solid lines and dotted lines indicate relationships and communication channels. However, sometimes these traditional structures are not adequate when the organization wants to aggressively examine or redesign work, workflow, and information systems. Direction and accountability become even more complicated when special cross-functional teams are set up for projects. The creation of a governance structure even applies if you want to make simple changes in how work is done or in who does what work. Assigning a project lead is not always adequate. Instead, setting up a group to provide direction may be more effective. The group can provide a platform for debate, be a vehicle for discussing issues, and generate recommendations to senior management. The people in the group can offer political savvy and support on particularly touchy issues. The important point is that the onus for leadership does not fall on one person but on an appointed group who can diffuse issues, act as a bellwether for new ideas, and communicate "off line" to identify resistance and gain support. The role of the governance group is

- To define the deliverable and the expected result

- To recommend or authorize the use of resources to do the work required to accomplish the mandate

- To surface factors that encumber progress, and to debate and recommend ways to eliminate or circumvent them

- To evaluate different solutions and recommend which one to purchase, implement, adopt, or support

- To guide and direct the efforts of work groups or teams on special assignment by providing them with a mission and with feedback

- To monitor milestones and timelines and take steps to keep projects on track

- To act as a panel of peers to hear concerns, mediate opposing views, and render opinions

The structure deals with questions such as, "Who has the right to veto?" "Who is responsible for the coordination?" "Who approves new policies and procedures?" "Who gets credit for the work and the ensuing results?"

A governance structure supplements and enhances leadership when:

- It facilitates decision making, that is, helps get decisions made quickly

- It facilitates debate and fosters problem solving, that is, legitimizes and enables having different perspectives heard when there are questions or unresolved issues, rather than avoiding the issues

- It does not censor opposing views, but provides a legitimate platform to hear and debate different ideas and opinions

- It provides direction and is seen by the organization as the source for vision, priorities, answers, and recommendations for how to proceed

Your current structure is not adequate if it does not do these things. A new or improved structure is helpful when the old one is inefficient because decisions take too long to make or implement, management is not timely in responding to concerns or requests, or workers feel there is no platform for arguing over ideas.

Governance structures can take different formats, such as "office of the president" and the use of program managers to provide a single point of contact. The following is an example of using a governance structure that goes outside the normal chain of command to support a major change. You can do something similar to support much smaller changes as well.

Here is a set of guidelines for modifying your current structure or creating a new one to better support decision making and collaboration. You can apply these guidelines to support ongoing work and special assignments.

TOOL 2.1: HOW TO DESIGN A GOVERNANCE STRUCTURE

Purpose

This set of guidelines will help you decide whether you require a new structure to make decisions and provide direction. If you do, it will walk you through the steps of creating one. The model given here is designed to help overcome problems with inefficiency and indecision. If you believe it would be helpful for you, continue.

How

Ask why you want a new or improved structure. Meet with your boss and others you think would benefit from a new model for making decisions. Explain what the purpose is. Discuss what you think would be the benefits and the types of pitfalls a new structure might help you avoid. As a group, identify the measures you will use to judge whether the new model made life easier or solved a problem.

A. With your boss and other people you think appropriate, identify three groups that represent different stakeholders:

1. Senior management. This can be your boss and/or your boss's boss. If possible include an administrative assistant or someone who has access to senior management's calendar. You will require this assistant's help in putting issues on the agenda for review or approval.

2. An advisory group. This should include you and your peers or internal customers. Look for people who depend on your group's work or who have a vested interest in your effectiveness.

3. The workers. These include your direct reports or a specially assigned team. These are the people who want feedback, approval, help resolving problems, and support for their ideas.

B. Define the roles, relationships, and expectations of each group.

1. Senior management is usually responsible for:

   a. Describing the mandate or deliverable

   b. Defining the measures or what change or outcome is expected that will be accepted as evidence of success

   c. Legitimizing the effort by stating to the larger organization how the structure functions and why it was created

   d. Reviewing and approving recommendations and actions

2. The advisory group's role is to

   a. Identify cross-functional dependencies, recognize dilemmas, and resolve problems

  b. Hear the workers' concerns, requests for resources, or need for approval to go ahead

  c. Provide input based on their perspective, needs, and requirements

  d. Test the organization's receptivity to new ideas

  e. Develop recommendations for senior management's consideration with a rationale for support

  f. Build support for the recommendations approved by senior management

  g. Mediate any disputes that may arise

 3. The employees' or team's role is to

  a. Do the work whether it includes meeting the usual deliverables or doing a special assignment

  b. Identify barriers they would like help handling

  c. Bring issues and recommendations to the advisory team for review and support

  d. Report on their progress

C. Call the first meeting of the advisory team.

 1. Develop an agenda noting what you want to accomplish

 2. Confirm an understanding of their role

 3. Identify the team's deliverables and measures of success

 4. Set up a meeting schedule frequent enough to keep people involved and be of value to the organization

 5. Develop a set of meeting guidelines all can accept (start on time, post agenda two days before the meeting to obtain input, frame the agenda in terms of accomplishments, everyone attend, and so forth)

D. Meet with senior management to confirm the advisory team's role and responsibilities and deliverables to confirm they agree.

E. Meet with the employees to explain the new structure and the protocol for bringing up issues, updating the advisory team, and so on.

Hint: As you design the structure, think about how it might help diffuse the power of certain individuals and harness the power of the group.

DULLES AIRPORT—
MAINTENANCE MANAGEMENT PROCESS

Leadership

The planning team determined it would take approximately three years to deliver on the promise of a more responsive yet cost-effective maintenance management process. The questions came up over who should lead the effort and how direction could be assured over the course of the project. It had been assumed that the director of maintenance and engineering or his direct report, the manager of the work order desk, would lead the effort. However, the planning team recommended a different approach that involved more stakeholders, was collaborative, and increased the odds that the project would achieve the sustained level of attention it required. The planning team saw the need for a new governance structure to assure direction was provided long-term, there was alignment with the airport's strategic planning process, and there was greater buy-in by the other departments dependent on maintenance (see Figure 2.2). This new governance structure would be a model for future cross-functional collaboration and would provide a template for how maintenance would be managed in the future.

Governance Structure

The planning team believed a new leadership model was required to change the way decisions about maintenance were made at the airport. In the past, decisions

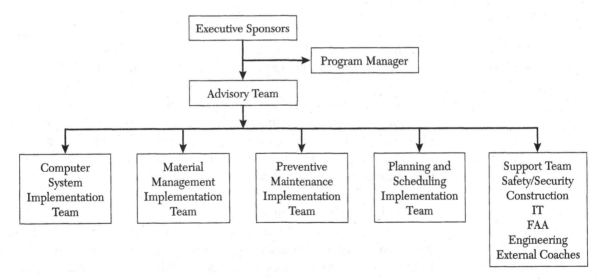

Figure 2.2. Governance Structure

related to maintenance were set aside because issues related to construction were given a higher priority. The planning team recommended:

1. The creation of an executive sponsorship team that consisted of the airport manager and his chief administrator. The role of the executive sponsorship team was to provide final approvals and to maintain communication with senior management, union leaders, and other managers at the airport.

2. The creation of a cross-functional advisory team with representatives from airport operations, concessions, an airline, purchasing, labor, HR, and maintenance, who collectively would provide counsel to the program manager, help formulate recommendations to the airport manager, recommend resources to actually implement a new system, develop the team charters for the specialty teams, and help resolve issues.

3. The appointment of a fully dedicated program manager from one of the shops in maintenance. The role of the program manager was to coordinate all of the activities involved in creating and deploying a new maintenance system, facilitate meetings with the advisory team, document all decisions and recommendations, and keep the executive sponsors informed.

4. The creation of a series of specialty teams who would be assigned specific deliverables.

But a governance structure alone will not provide adequate direction unless it has official endorsement by senior management and operating protocols.

ENDORSEMENT AND LEGITIMACY

The governance structure must be seen as legitimate. The actions and recommendations of temporary groups are frequently seen as outside the norm and, therefore, lack the legitimacy of those from more permanent departments. Yet temporary groups require that their decisions and recommendations be recognized as legitimate. Gaining legitimacy is especially troublesome in organizations that follow a very hierarchical approach to decisions about work priorities and the use of human and financial resources. Program managers, cross-functional teams, and people on special projects almost always produce recommendations to change how work is done and who does it. These recommendations directly impact department managers who may be of higher status in the organization as defined by the organizational chart. Cross-functional teams, in particular, require that people be assigned to them either full-time or part-time if they are to accomplish their mandate. Yet managers in the line organization may have already decided how to use their resources, so expecting them to release staff to work on other assignments is difficult.

The behaviors that signal legitimacy at a minimum are senior management making public announcements to those parts of the organization expected to be affected and to provide support. Management must say explicitly it supports a project, a process, or a set of governing principles. Operating protocols can help management define the roles, responsibilities, and relationships of new governance structures with the established chain of command.

OPERATIONAL PROTOCOLS

Protocols are a combination of good manners and commonly accepted conventions. They are frequently referred to as "the way we do business" or "that's how things get done." Protocols become evident when you look at how families and friends entertain. Some hosts expect guests to help clear the table and participate in the clean-up. Other hosts would be insulted at any offer of help. Some hosts expect guests to bring wine, side dishes, or dessert to go with the meal. Other hosts plan every aspect of the meal and would prefer guests bring nothing. Some hosts place salt and pepper on the table, others preseason the food and are insulted if you ask to alter the taste. Knowing and following these little social rules helps maintain civility, friendships, and family harmony.

Organizations, too, develop protocols that evolve over time, are rarely written down, and are frequently not recognized unless violated by someone. Examples are

- The sequence and the manner in which certain managers or departments are officially informed of major decisions
- When, by whom, and where the union leadership is informed of changes possibly affecting the rank and file
- The way some people are informally informed before any manager makes an announcement or a message is sent to the rest of the organization
- How resources are re-deployed or reassigned to special projects outside of the managers' scope of responsibilities
- Whether or not agenda are produced and followed during regular meetings, who prepares the agenda, and how changes are made
- Always having coffee, juice, and sweet rolls available for early morning meetings and cookies in the mid-afternoon for all-day sessions
- Giving gifts and other tokens of appreciation to teams assigned to special projects
- Supporting officially endorsed corporate humanitarian efforts
- Selling your child's cookies, calendars, candy, wrapping paper, or magazine subscriptions to co-workers

However, not all protocols support performance. Some organizations have established ways of doing business that support inaction, are counterproductive, and can even polarize departments against one another, for example, being expected to include certain people who are known to stall, table ideas, or take groups off task by conjecturing about inane possibilities. When work is not getting done or there are new expectations about how it should be done or when new initiatives are deployed or the organization wants to make major changes to how work gets done, it may be necessary to create new protocols. Therefore, it is important to identify what the current protocols are, ask how well they support innovation and collaboration, and, based on the answers, either change or supplement them to support the behaviors required to obtain the desired results.

DULLES AIRPORT

Formal Communication

The advisory team and program manager saw a need to formally communicate what the project was about, how the governance structure operated, and what the responsibilities were of the program manager and the specialized implementation teams. The advisory team believed the airport manager had to stand up and tell the story, state his expectations about everyone's support, and publicly endorse the legitimacy of the advisory team and program manager. With this need in mind, the advisory team developed a protocol about how to formally announce the project to all the people in key positions, keep them informed, and give them a mechanism to express their concerns and raise issues. The program manager, with help from vendors and HR, prepared a presentation for the airport manager that he could deliver to senior management, the other airport directors, the union leadership, and the other supervisors and managers at the airport. The next step was to develop an ongoing communication plan and put it on the larger project calendar. The program manager flagged the recurring meetings between the airport manager and senior management, the airport directors, and the union. The program manager wanted to do everything he could to keep the project on the minds of senior management. The program manager put it on his "to do" list to give the airport manager up-to-date information on the status of the project and any issues that needed to be resolved by him and the others.

TOOLS AND TECHNIQUES

Here are four commonly used techniques for supplementing leadership by developing new protocols about how decisions get made and communicated, how work gets done, and who is responsible for what part. The techniques are best used in combination, as none of them can replace leadership, but can only support it.

1. Cross-functional diagrams—a diagram that shows who is responsible for specific tasks and decisions and the sequence of those actions. It can also show the flow of communication, such as who originates it and where it goes.

2. Governing principles—a series of statements that describe expected behaviors and how group members will relate to each other and people outside of the group. The principles served as a code of conduct.

3. Operating guidelines—a document that describes how decisions are made and by whom and how individuals and groups will seek approvals and keep each other informed on an ongoing basis to assure work progresses in a timely fashion.

4. RASCI charts[2]—a chart that shows for every task who is responsible for doing it, who is authorized to approve work or expenditures, who provides administrative or technical support, who should and can provide counsel, and who should be kept informed.

All of these techniques define expected behaviors. The cross-functional diagram and RASCI charts assign roles and show relationships. Cross-functional charts add the element of sequence. Governing principles and operating guidelines formalize protocols. More importantly, the use of these techniques is an opportunity to solicit concerns and facilitate dialogue about expectations. The actual documents help communicate the expected behaviors and who is responsible for what to people outside of the group.

Here are the guidelines for all tools. Collectively they can help you clarify roles, relationships, and responsibilities to assure people and groups receive the direction they require to be effective. You can print these and modify them to better suit your requirements.

TOOL 2.2: HOW TO DEVELOP AND USE CROSS-FUNCTIONAL CHARTS

Purpose

This technique clarifies roles and relationships and it shows the sequence of activities and who communicates with whom and when.

How

In collaboration with the work group or people who will be assigned to do the work:

A. Identify the types of tasks or roles that have to be done.

B. Put each task on a self-stick note.

Figure 2.3. Sample Cross-Functional Chart

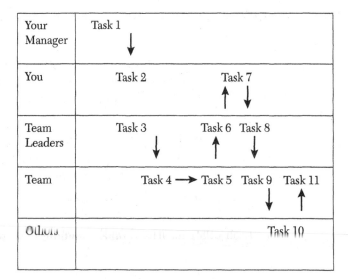

| Your Manager | Task 1 |
| Team | Task 4 → Task 5 Task 9 Task 11 |

C. Put them in some sequence, like the order things will be done in a process, all the things that happen once a request is received from a customer or manager, or all the things that happen before, during, and after a regularly scheduled meeting.

D. Create a table of rows using either a word processing spreadsheet or graphic software (see Figure 2.3). At the beginning of each row, list the person or group that is expected to play a role. The role might be to provide information, perform a task, review or approve work, or make decisions. Include yourself, your manager, the team or work group members, and other managers or departments who will be affected by the work or should be consulted in some way, such as legal, human resources, accounting, union officials, and others (see Figure 2.3).

E. Place each note in the row of the person or group responsible for doing it.

F. Create additional notes to show where one person's task acts as an input and triggers someone else to do something.

G. Show which tasks occur concurrently by placing them one below the other.

H. Draw arrows showing how the completion of each task becomes an input to another task that may be done by the same person or group or go to another person or group.

I. Pilot-test your understanding of who does what and when. Use what you learn to modify each person's responsibilities as required.

Hint: Use this technique to identify tasks that no longer add value. It can help you streamline your processes and make them more efficient.

TOOL 2.3: HOW TO DEVELOP GOVERNING PRINCIPLES, PROTOCOLS, AND GROUND RULES

Purpose

This technique is best used when you want to raise awareness as to the importance of the group adhering to a set of behaviors, because those behaviors engender trust and collaboration and foster goal accomplishment. The protocols or rules are written and formally endorsed, unlike the informal protocols that evolve over time. Everyone should have a voice in creating them.

How

One group may draft the principles; then other groups can read and modify them until consensus is reached. Once the list is formally adopted, it can be disseminated to everyone affected by it.

A. As a group, brainstorm those situations in which you think protocols will help prevent misunderstandings or friction. Include things like these:

1. When and how often the group might convene to discuss issues

2. When an issue surfaces how long people have to bring it to the group for resolution

3. How decisions are made, collectively or by specific individuals

4. How everyone will be kept informed of decisions, upcoming events, and so on

5. Expected values like honesty, dealing with people directly rather than behind their backs, committing to help each other succeed, treating each other with respect, keeping issues within the group and not going outside with gossip, and any others

B. Share the list with others you think might care and could offer feedback or suggestions.

C. Once the group accepts the list, have everyone sign it as a way of showing their public commitment.

D. Laminate the list, frame it, and hang it where it can be seen.

E. Periodically, put the list on the agenda and set time aside for the group to discuss if and how it is helping them do the work before them and what changes they would like to make, if any.

Hint: Link the behavior to the organization's espoused value and competency statements if you have them.

TOOL 2.4: HOW TO DEVELOP OPERATING GUIDELINES AND PROCEDURES

Purpose

This technique is similar to the governing principles, but is better used to define discrete behaviors for informing people, gaining approvals, and assigning resources. Some examples might be the names of people who should be informed before a general announcement is made; the name of the person who has the right to override a decision and how that is done so as to prevent confusion; when certain decisions should be made by different people; and how the decisions are identified and the person is informed. The guidelines are much more operational or procedural in nature than the governing principles, which are more about personal conduct. They are usually created when there has been confusion about how to accomplish a task efficiently. The guidelines should make it easier to hand over a task to the next person. They should help keep the group on task and not be delayed because they are waiting or debating who does what and when.

How

With your team and representatives from those groups it must work with to obtain information and have work reviewed or approved:

A. Identify those events or circumstances where work is held up or misunderstandings occur.

B. Together, create a set of procedures that explains how the interface should optimally happen.

C. Next, identify those circumstances that would prevent you from doing the procedure. Identify the exceptions.

D. Together create a set of procedures to handle the exceptions or unusual circumstances.

E. Try the guidelines out.

F. Periodically meet to discuss what is and is not working and modify the procedures so they better serve your needs.

Hint: Try not to add another layer of approvals. The goal is to streamline decisions and clarify accountability, not add complexity. You also want people to get off the fence and step up to making decisions.

Here is an example of how the airport used three of the techniques to supplement and enhance leadership.

DULLES AIRPORT

Because the maintenance program presented an opportunity to model a new way of managing that required an unprecedented level of cross-functional collaboration, a new set of protocols was required to prevent hurt feelings, misunderstandings, or distractions over who was authorized to do what. Three techniques were used to help define and communicate roles and relationships:

1. Governing principles
2. Cross-functional charts
3. Operating guidelines

Governing Principles[3]

The planning team created a draft of governing principles, a list of behaviors expected of everyone involved in maintenance at the airport. The advisory team finalized them. The governing principles were shared with every subteam and with the other supervisors in maintenance and engineering. Here is an excerpt from the twenty-one governing principles developed by the planning team and later adopted by the airport manager, the program manager, and the advisory team:

- I, as a member of the team, commit to operate under these governing principles
- Safety is not an option; I will ensure all actions support safety/security/risk reduction
- I will do everything I can to keep co-workers, partners, and customers from failing
- I demand mutual respect, will try to understand the perspective of each person, and will treat everyone regardless of position or background with respect and dignity
- This is my facility; I will be proud of the job I do and will let it show in the quality of the work I perform
- I will make all decisions related to the purchase of materials or services as if the expenditure were mine

Cross-Functional Chart

The program manager was still uncomfortable with his role and level of responsibility. On the surface it appeared he was expected to tell managers higher than him in the organization to release people to work on the project. The problem was even more complicated because his boss was on the advisory team and he felt it inappropriate to tell his boss what to do. To help him sort through his concerns and gain commitment from the airport manager about what his actual level of authority was, he created a cross-functional chart. On the chart he listed the executive sponsors (airport manager and chief administrator), himself as the program manager, the advisory team, the special implementation teams, and other stakeholders such as union leaders and managers outside of maintenance. He then put down the tasks that he saw were required and assigned them to himself, the executive sponsor, the advisory team, and others (see Figure 2.4). He showed the chart to the advisory team for their input. Next he met with the airport manager and the two of them used the chart to talk through actual examples. Together they arrived at a mutual understanding of roles and responsibilities.

Operating Guidelines

The program manager and the advisory team felt it was important for the airport manager to legitimize certain decisions or actions. They believed sending an email to the other supervisors and managers about what would be happening would not create the level of support required unless the airport manager somehow indicated that the recommendations met with his approval. The program manager and advisory team came up with a way for the airport manager to formally communicate his approval. After each advisory team meeting, the program manager would send an email with the attached minutes of the meeting to the executive sponsors. However, in the email itself the program manager would flag those items requiring official approval. The airport manager, given he did approve, sent back an email within twenty-four hours saying that he approved the suggested actions or decisions. The airport manager's email was sent to the program manager, the advisory team members, and all other managers and supervisors at the airport.

Here is another technique you can use to supplement and enhance leadership, the RASCI chart.

TOOL 2.5: HOW TO DEVELOP AND USE RASCI CHARTS

Purpose

This technique is best used when there is disagreement or a lack of clarity over who is responsible for what.

How

    A. Identify and involve the people on your team or other co-workers who depend on clear direction to do their work.

    B. With your team, create a matrix or table in a word processing or spreadsheet software. Across the top list the names of key players who

Maintenance Excellence

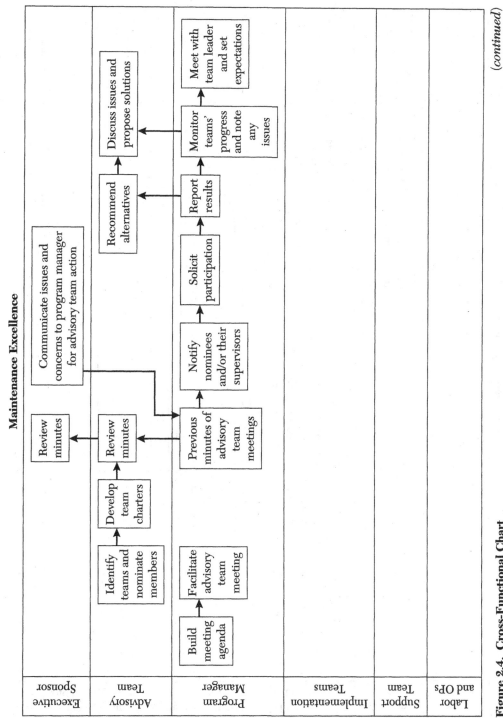

Figure 2.4. Cross-Functional Chart

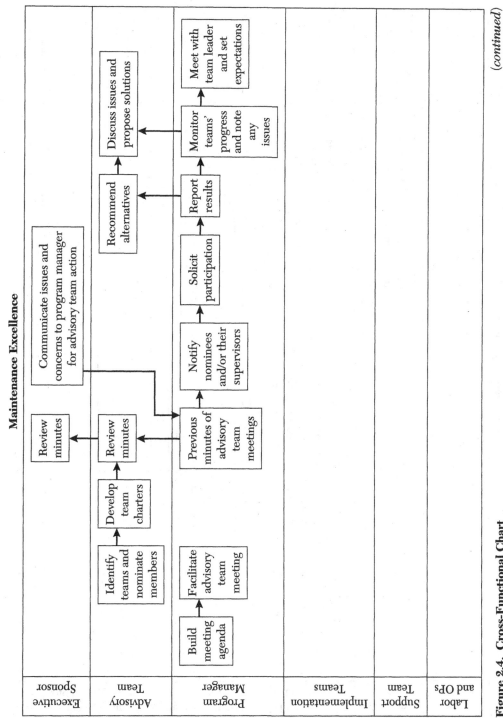

(continued)

Maintenance Management

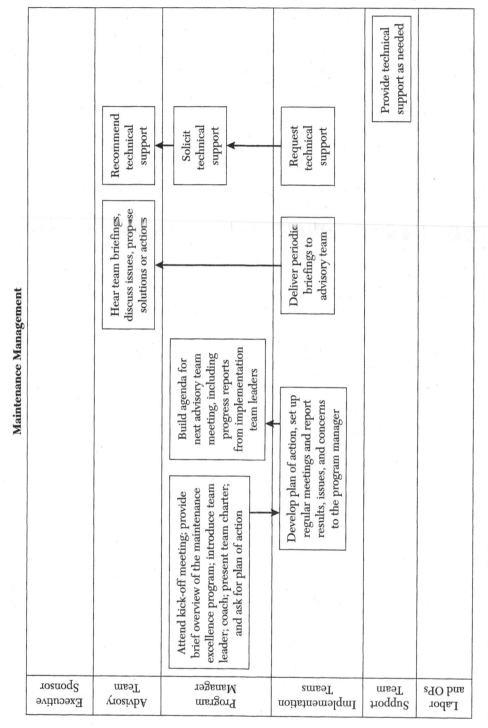

Figure 2.4. Cross-Functional Chart (Continued)

Figure 2.5. Sample RASCI Chart

	Person 1	Person 2	Person 3	Person n
Task 1	R	I	A	S
Task 2	I	R	A	C
Task 3	R	C	A	S
Task n				

should have some role in fulfilling the mandate of the team or work group. Down the side list the actions or tasks that must be completed to accomplish the work (see Figure 2.5). Be as complete as possible.

C. Together, for each task place a letter (RASCI) under the name of the person who:

1. Is responsible—the person who is ultimately responsible that the work be completed. This may be the person who actually does the work or directs others to do the work.

2. Has approval—the person who has the legitimate authority to approve the adequacy of the deliverable (work), budgets, resource allocations, assignments, purchases, and so forth.

3. Can provide support—the people who can provide administrative services or coordinate the logistics.

4. Can provide counsel—the people with technical expertise, such as labor relations, legal, quality assurance, and others who can help teams fulfill their mandates.

5. Should be informed—the people who need to know the status of the work or the decisions that were made, whether it be a matter of courtesy or to help them better schedule their own work or the work of others.

D. Share the form with everyone whose name appears on the form and any others who may have a legitimate voice in how work is done to get their input.

E. Use what you learn to modify the form.

F. Begin to use the form as a guide and note where there are omissions or oversights.

G. Modify the form as you learn what does and does not work.

Hint: Use the chart to resolve disputes or confusion over roles, responsibilities, and relationships.

TIPS

1. When you create project plans, include a line for governance and communication. Expand the time frame to beyond one year, certainly beyond the initial implementation so you can find out whether there were any unforeseen side effects.

2. Keep your work on management's and other stakeholders' agenda.

3. Develop a master calendar that shows when your management is meeting and when other key events occur.

4. Ask your manager or sponsor to represent your work at meetings and support keeping updates on the calendar.

5. Assume there is space on the agenda to hear about your work and send an email to the person preparing the agenda asking for three to seven minutes. Attach a headline or brief statement on the topic.

6. Just prior to the meetings or events, prepare a brief update on what has been accomplished to date in notes or a presentation format such as PowerPoint®. Give the updates to your boss, sponsor, or a representative of management to present on your behalf.

7. Meet with people who have led other major projects and ask what difficulties they may have had that caused ill feelings or delays due to lack of support and resistance from other groups. Use the information to develop some protocols to help you avoid the same difficulties in the future.

SUMMARY

Leadership depends on specific behaviors that reinforce or cue others to act in certain ways. However, in the absence of strong leadership you can provide direction through the design of governance structures and the formalization of operational protocols so people at all levels are continually reminded of what is important, where the organization is headed, and what's required of them.

WHERE TO LEARN MORE

Here are some books to help you provide direction for others.

Hupp, T., Polak, C., and Westgaard, O. *Designing Work Groups, Jobs, and Work Flow* (San Francisco, CA: Jossey-Bass, 1995). Pages 80 through 83 have a very nice job aid to help you develop a cross-functional chart.

Damelo, R. *The Basics of Process Mapping* (New York: Productivity Inc., 1996). This is a good little reference and about sixty-five pages in length.

Panza, C. M. *Picture This . . . Your Function, Your Company* (Morristown, NJ: Panza, CMP Associates, 1989).

NOTES

1. Smith, M.E. Implementing Organization Change: Correlates of Success and Failure, *Performance Improvement Quarterly, 15*(1), 2002. Published by the Learning Systems Institute, Florida State University, in cooperation with the International Society for Performance Improvement.
2. RASCI Charts were developed by the Department of Defense and originally called Linear Responsibility Charts. They were used to clarify roles and responsibilities of people and functions assigned to large projects. The name "RASCI" evolved as the charts were adopted by defense contractors.
3. There were a total of twenty-one governing principles generated by the group. Only an excerpt is given here to illustrate the tone and intent of the document.

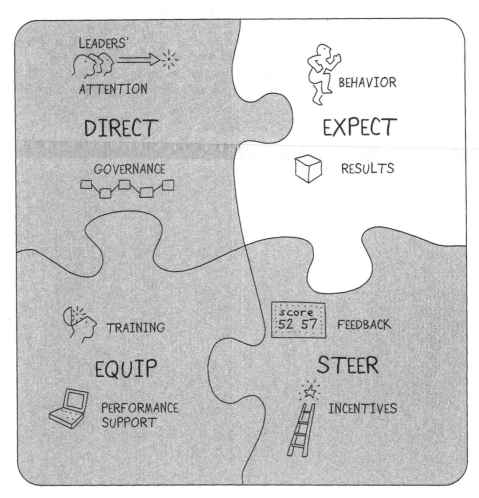

Figure 3.1. Leadership Roles

Lynn Kearny, CPT, Graphic Recorder

Chapter 3

How to Set Expectations

What do you want from me?

Once you have determined the direction of the organization and the work unit, the next job is to identify and communicate what you expect of your people, individually and collectively. The information that most communicates what you expect comes from what you promised customers and from what you will use as evidence that your promise is being fulfilled. Therefore, this chapter is about how to identify deliverables, customers, and performance measures, as this is the information that shapes people's behavior. Here are some definitions that will help you to understand and communicate expectations:

- A *job* is a collection of duties that constitute the total work assignment of a worker.

- A *duty* refers to a large segment of work or a major area of responsibility and consists of several related tasks, for example, a person may have the duty to maintain equipment or to train others on how to operate the equipment. The term duty is also used to infer a moral obligation, for example, a parent's duty to provide for the children, a citizen's duty to vote, and a supervisor's duty to provide guidance and support to subordinates.

- A *task* is a discrete unit of work. It usually comprises the logical and necessary steps in the performance of a duty and has an identifiable beginning and end.

- A *role* is an assigned perspective or attitude that goes beyond the normal job duties. For example, a person who has the job of purchasing agent may be asked to serve in the role of a technical advisor to a task force developing specifications to qualify vendors.[1]

- *Measures* are the behaviors, attributes, or results that you use as evidence that people are performing their jobs and that they are proficient and productive.

- *Proficiency* is one set of measures and is about the ability to do the work. People are proficient when they can do the job and produce deliverables that satisfy the need under normal conditions.

- *Productivity* is another set of measures and is about how much gets done and with how many resources within a given time frame. People are productive when they produce a sufficient number of deliverables or outputs within the expected time frame using the expected number of resources (time, materials, money, and so forth).

- *Performance* is another set of measures and is about the worth of the results that were achieved and the integrity of the behaviors used to do the work.

- *Measuring* is the purposeful act of gathering information to find out whether the behaviors, attributes, and results you want to see are sufficiently present for you to determine whether people are proficient, productive, and performing.

- However, to know whether people are proficient, productive, or performing you have to *compare* what you discover to something, such as *standards*, *goals*, or some *past measure*. Whatever you use as a point of comparison, you should decide before you measure.

PERFORMANCE IMPROVEMENT

From a performance improvement perspective, the presence of clear expectations is a key predictor of performance. Similarly, when people are unclear about what is expected or there is disagreement on what the objectives are of the job or task, and what will be used to judge proficiency, performance suffers. First-line managers and supervisors are in the best position to communicate expectations; however, they frequently assume someone else did it. The ability to set expectations is made more difficult when managers and supervisors get conflicting or ambiguous messages from their superiors.

COMMON MISSTEPS

Here are some common mistakes managers and supervisors make:

1. They assume that people know what they are supposed to produce and for whom.

2. They assume people understand on what basis their performance is being measured.

3. They assume that what is being measured drives the appropriate behaviors and generates the desired results.

4. They believe everyone knows and agrees on the criteria used to judge whether or not the work is of sufficient quantity, quality, and timeliness to be of value to those who depend on it.

5. They fail to communicate what is expected in terms of performance and confirm that the communication was understood.

WHAT SETS EXPECTATIONS

Job Descriptions

For most individuals, job descriptions and hiring criteria begin the process of defining and communicating expectations. People expect their job descriptions to be accurate. When people are hired and discover that what is expected is significantly different from what they first understood about the job, they become confused and the organization risks not getting the level of performance it requires. Therefore, you should find out what information is contained in the job descriptions and confirm that they set appropriate expectations. Unfortunately, some job descriptions do not specify objectives, deliverables, or measures. Instead, HR usually expects you to communicate what the objectives, deliverables, and measures are.

Purpose

Sometimes it helps just to ask why the organization even created your unit and the job positions in it. There must have been an expectation that something would be better accomplished or different as a result of having your work unit and the job positions within it.

Customer Expectations

It can also help to confirm your understanding of just who your customers are and who depends on or benefits from your unit's outputs. Knowing why you exist and who relies on the work you produce helps you to determine what your unit's objectives are. The assumption is that the objectives were derived from the goals for the department or division; however, department goals are not always easy to translate into objectives for smaller work units or individuals. Customers can add clarity and purpose.

Deliverables

Managers and supervisors often overlook the importance of periodically questioning just what their deliverables are and who depends on them. It is easier for people who directly interface with external customers, such as sales, or those who manufacture goods to understand what they do and for whom. People in other types of jobs may feel they are too removed from top management or customers and lack sight of their roles in the organization. The concept of an internal customer is also not readily understood, because people do not always see their work as part of a larger process. Yet, being clear about your deliverables and customer is essential to being able to evaluate your people's performance, improve your work processes, and act as a champion for your group.

To reconfirm just what your group's deliverables are, start by asking who your customers are. Next, ask what your group produces that those customers rely on; what do they require of your group to meet their needs or to do their work? Include physical items, information, and emotional factors. Emotional deliverables include a sense of confidence and due diligence, especially if your group performs an audit or quality assurance function. Here are some examples:

Shipping Clerk. On the surface, it looks like a shipping clerk only interfaces with drivers who work for the freight companies. The clerk, however, completes paperwork and enters data into a computer that is perhaps used by accounts receivable for billing customers, customer service for tracking shipments, the organization's website so customers can track the status of their own deliveries, and so forth. A shipping clerk's deliverables include confidence that merchandise was loaded correctly and on the right truck and data used by accounting, customer service, inventory management, and others. The clerk's internal customers then are accounting, customer service, inventory control, and perhaps others.

Maintenance. The maintenance crew maintains and repairs all of the heating, air conditioning, plumbing, electrical, and mechanical systems within a facility. Their deliverables include functioning systems and data about those systems' performance. Their customers are the people who work in the facilities, their co-workers who operate the systems, the facility manager, and perhaps purchasing, who contracts for the acquisition of new equipment and supplies.

Merchandising. The people who work in merchandising come up with ideas (their deliverables) on how to best position products at the point of sale, in a store, catalogue, or website, compared to the competition. Their ideas may include the store floor plans, where and how to place products on shelves in retail outlets, and what related products to suggest when people buy online. Their customers include product managers, sales managers, and retail outlet managers.

TOOL 3.1: HOW TO IDENTIFY DELIVERABLES

Purpose

This guideline is designed to help your work unit gain an understanding of what they produce and why. It can help you determine whether your understanding of your deliverables is the same as what others in the organization think.

How

Start the process with your own people. Perhaps ask someone from training or HR to help. Eventually involve someone who represents the departments that rely on your work unit's outputs, top management, and other stakeholders who have a vested interest in your work and how it is executed. As you answer each question, ask yourself:

- Have I communicated this to my people?
- How can I use the answers to help better communicate my expectations?

A. Discuss the following questions:

1. What is the purpose of the jobs in our work unit? Why were we created?
2. What do we produce that others rely on?
3. Who in the organization depends on our outputs to do their work?
4. If our jobs did not exist, who would be affected and in what way?
5. Who are the customers of our outputs or deliverables? How do customers use what we do or create?
6. If we serve different customers, who are they and what do we provide those customers?
7. If individuals or teams have specific assignments or projects to work on, what are the expected deliverables and who are the customers?
8. Who in the organization uses information we produce to make decisions? Quality assurance? Finance? Upper management? Others?

B. Try drawing a picture that shows where your group fits in the process of producing things that are used by other groups, both inside and outside of the organization. In the picture show (1) the groups that rely on your people for information, direction, support, or things and (2) the groups you rely on for information, direction, support, or things so you can do your work, as you are someone else's customer as well.

C. Next, with representatives from customers, management, or other stakeholders, ask

1. If my group did not exist, who would be affected?
2. What would other groups in the organization have to provide or produce for the organization to deliver its products and services?

D. Share your group's answers to the first set of questions to find out whether your perspective is the same as that of your customers, upper management, and peers.

E. Based on the answers to the above questions, define:

1. The objectives of the unit and the jobs that make up the unit.

2. The group's deliverables.

3. The group's customers.

Hint: Begin to think about the factors that you, your people, and your customers use to judge the quality and usefulness of your work. This is valuable information for deciding what to measure.

Here is an example of how another group came to understand where it fit in the organization and who its customers were.

MAINTENANCE

The maintenance department was asked who their customers were. The question was met with blank stares. Historically, the people in the maintenance department only focused on the equipment they maintained. The idea that others in the laboratory relied on the equipment they maintained to do their work was known, but not really discussed. No one had ever thought of asking how the lab was affected either by how maintenance did its work or by the results of its work. The maintenance crews maintained autoclaves, large drive-in freezers, and boilers, the equipment the scientists relied heavily on to do their experiments. The scientists did not always understand the capability of the equipment and sometimes did things that either exceeded its capacity or jeopardized the functioning of other equipment. When asked, the scientists said they expected maintenance to keep the equipment up and running and to be told what they might do to better assure it was not compromised because of something they did.

The crews in the maintenance department never thought that purchasing was a customer. Instead, they thought they were just victims of the purchasing department's decisions about what equipment and supplies to buy. It was when asked who their customers were that they came to understand that they had more information about how equipment functioned and what was required to maintain it than anyone else. This information was valuable to the scientists in the lab and to the people in purchasing.

WHERE TO FIND MEASURES

What you measure usually comes from:

- The goals and objectives of the work unit and individuals for the year or for a specific assignment
- Your and your group's deliverables or outputs
- Your customers' (internal and external) expectations of you and your group
- Your own interest in evaluating someone's performance, perhaps to identify development needs, performance issues, or promotional readiness

Typically, managers and supervisors measure the quantity, quality, timeliness, and accuracy of the work produced and the results that ensue. However, you must decide why you want to measure. It could be that you want to know more about the proficiency, productivity, or performance of your group, specific individuals, or a new process you put in place. Whatever the reason, you should decide on the questions you want to answer through the process of measuring. For example, do you want to confirm (1) that someone knows, can do, or is doing something or that he or she gets along with others; (2) that a new process saved time, reduced errors, or reduced costs; or (3) that customers are receiving what they want? Your questions lead you to an appropriate combination of measures. Here are some examples.

CUSTOMER SERVICE REPRESENTATIVES (CSR)

The deliverable might be to respond to customer calls. The objectives might be that, given a sufficient number of calls from customers, a working telephone system, and online access to customer files, the CSR will:

- Achieve and sustain the average call handling time
- Resolve 80 percent of customer issues on the first call
- Only escalate calls when the issue is outside one's expertise or the customer is difficult

The measures might include:

- Average number of calls handled within a specific number of work hours
- Average call handling time
- Average number of calls not resolved in first contact (resulting in a call-back)
- Average number of calls appropriately escalated to technical support, team lead, or supervisor

Evaluating CSR performance based on the types of calls coming into the center from customers (to make a purchase, complain, or check the status of an order) is not appropriate, as CSRs have no control over the types of calls that come in or how they are routed. However, measuring the types of calls that come in during a shift or to the work unit is good information to have, as it helps you spot trends and make sure call center staff are appropriately equipped to handle the more common calls.

FIELD SERVICE TECHNICIAN (FST)

The deliverables might include servicing customers' equipment, preventive maintenance and repairs, and selling replacement parts and service agreements. The objectives might be, given adequate training, appropriate and working tools, the FST will:

- Handle a specific number of routine service calls per week
- Generate a specific amount of revenue from the sale of parts or service
- Keep customers satisfied so they purchase service contracts
- Handle all routine service calls in one visit

The measures might include:

- Average number of service calls handled
- Average time per call
- Customer satisfaction ratings
- Average number (dollar volume) of parts replaced
- Average dollar volume from the sale of new parts, services, or service agreements

A measure like the ratio of warranty to non-warranty calls is not appropriate for individual technicians, as they have no control over this, but it is appropriate information for the work unit and quality assurance. Also, measuring why customers call for service can give you a better handle on what your technicians require in terms of skills, work procedures, and materials.

FLOOR/SHIFT SUPERVISOR

The deliverable of the work unit might be to produce goods or render a service and to assure adequate coverage. The objectives might be, given a trained crew, working equipment, production goals, and adequate materials, the supervisor will:

- Meet the production quota and not exceed scrap rates
- Keep labor costs within budget
- Avoid employee complaints or labor grievances

  The measures might include:

- Actual amount produced
- Percent of product within standard or amount of scrap
- Overall labor rate and percent for overtime
- Employee retention rate
- Amount of tardiness, absenteeism, or complaints (from employees and customers)
- Number of performance appraisals conducted and the quality of those appraisals

The supervisor may not control the skill mix of employees, but he or she may want to assess their skills. Having the right people, with the right level of skills and with the right equipment, is a joint responsibility of human resources, top management, and the supervisor.

WHAT TO MEASURE

People should know what is being measured. You can measure at any of several levels:

- *Output or deliverable* level—this usually involves measuring quantity, volume, timeliness, number of errors, amount of rework, and usefulness of what was produced. These are also measures of proficiency and productivity.
- At the *process* level—this usually includes measuring efficiency, cost, and resource consumption. This, too, is a measure of proficiency, as people who are less proficient tend to consume more resources, including their own and other people's time for guidance and coaching.
- At the *outcome* level—this usually includes satisfaction (employee, customer, supplier, and investor), performance (product, process, and people), finance (cash flow, return on investment, and the like), and compliance (the number and size of regulatory citations and fines).

• At the *aftereffect* level—this usually includes the quality of customer, employee, and partner relationships and avoidance of shifting costs to others or into the future.

The following tool is designed to help you evaluate the usefulness of your current measures.

TOOL 3.2: HOW TO EVALUATE YOUR CURRENT USE OF MEASURES

Purpose

This guideline looks at your current measures and at how useful they are at helping you set expectations.

How

With your people, answer the following questions:

A. What do we measure now?

1. Outputs, such as quantity and volume?

2. Quality, such as usefulness, timeliness, meets standard, and so forth?

3. Process efficiency and reliability, like the amount of resources consumed or overall cycle time?

4. Results or outcomes, in terms of dollars, customer satisfaction, acceptance or adoption by others, market penetration, or goal accomplishment?

5. Other measures?

B. What information do we rely on to measure?

1. People's opinion?

2. Silence is good news?

3. Complaints?

4. Information in reports that come out regularly?

5. Information from time clocks or other systems that can track time and volume?

6. Information from auditors (internal and external), customers, peers, or others?

C. How do we get the data on which to base our decision that people are proficient, productive, and performing?

1. From production reports?

2. From customer or employee surveys?

3. From customer or co-worker complaints?

4. By observing the work being performed?

5. By checking the product of the work done?

6. From a system that tracks time and volume?

7. Other ways?

D. How do we use the data?

   1. To let people know how well they are doing?

   2. To identify who needs help or what is or is not working?

   3. To schedule resources or assignments?

   4. Other ways?

E. What do we use for comparison?

   1. Past or historic data?

   2. Performance targets or goals?

   3. Industry standards?

   4. Other expectations?

F. Do the current measures provide sufficient information to communicate what is expected and to help others stay focused on the behaviors and results that matter?

G. What could we do differently to better measure and use what we learn to help people be more productive?

Hint: The important things are to measure and to be willing to change what you measure or how you go about it should the process fail to help you make better decisions.

JOBS AND MEASURES

How you look at a job affects the measures you use to judge proficiency, productivity, or performance. Figure 3.2 shows three ways to look at jobs and how each one suggests what to measure.

As the figure shows, you can classify jobs in terms of the type of work that is done, such as piecework, procedural work, process work, mental or intellectual work, or relationship work. Most jobs do one type of work.

Type of Work Performed

Some jobs produce a product through *piecework*. Some require following a well-prescribed *procedure*. Some jobs are actually *processes,* like project management and product development. They incorporate a series of steps or activities that lead to some outcome. Still other jobs require *mental calculation,* the analysis of numerical, scientific, technical, and descriptive data; drawing conclusions and making judgments. Finally, some jobs are all about entering

Figure 3.2. Three Ways to Measure Job Performance	View 1: Type of Work Performed	View 2: The Skills and Knowledge Required	View 3: Amount of Variance or Predictability
	• Piecework • Procedural work • Process work • Mental or intellectual work • Relationship work	• Technical, scientific, or professional skills and knowledge • Relationship management skills and knowledge • Organization and administration skills and knowledge • Self-management skills and knowledge	• Routine to not routine • Predictable to unpredictable • Prescribed to ambiguous

into and sustaining *relationships,* such as account manager, community relationship manager, lobbyist, liaison, employee or labor relations. Ways to measure each type of work are listed below.

Piecework

- Error rate—on average how much does and does not meet the set standard
- Quantity—on average how many pieces are done within a specific time period, whether by count, weight, or volume
- Quality—on average how many pieces meet the standard or possess an attribute the organization values
- Time—how long it takes on average to do a piece
- Timeliness—on average whether the work was done in time to be useful

Procedural Work

- Compliance—on average how often people follow the procedures
- Quality—on average how many outputs met the standard
- Quantity—on average how much is done within a specific time frame
- Time—on average how long it takes to complete the procedure
- Timeliness—on average whether the work was done in time to be useful

Process Work

- Cycle time—the average overall time to complete the process
- Efficiency—the ratio of time at task to actual cycle time
- Goal accomplishment—how much was achieved

- Resource consumption—the average number of resources (people's time, system's time, materials, and so forth) consumed
- Resource cost—the average cost of the resources consumed
- Rework—the average amount of time spent doing rework
- Quantity—the number of projects or processes being handled and the quantity of outputs of those processes
- Timeliness—meeting deadlines
- Waiting—the average amount of time spent on waiting for approvals, reviews, materials, and so on

Mental or Intellectual Work

- Acceptance—the number of experts who agree with the recommendations or findings
- Accuracy—the number of errors in judgment compared to the number of recommendations made
- Adoption—the degree to which a recommendation is supported, endorsed, and followed through on by others
- Concurrent validation—the presence of other similar results
- Goal accomplishment—the consequences from having implemented the recommendations or acted on the findings
- Quantity—the number of ideas or recommendations generated compared to the number that are adopted and produce the expected results

Relationship Work

- Acceptance—the number of endorsements acquired, the number of times customers request the person specifically and cite his or her work as good, the frequency with which others want to be with the person, whether the data are anecdotal or derived from a customer satisfaction survey, the number of people in agreement with the person's ideas or the amount of cooperation or support the person can get
- Goal accomplishment—whether the person was able to obtain sufficient support for an idea so that it could be acted on or implemented
- Teamwork—how effective the team is and whether or not people ask for a person to be on their team
- Timeliness—how quickly the person can gain access to resources, decision makers, and so forth, whether the evidence is time or the number of efforts; how quickly the person can get others to commit to a purchase, idea, or course of action

Thinking about the type of work performed helps surface assumptions about what information can be used to measure proficiency or productivity. Proficiency is about ability, and productivity is about how much is done and how much energy is consumed in doing it. People are *proficient* when they can do the job under normal conditions. They are *productive* when they produce the desired deliverables with the expected level of resources, including time, money, and materials.

Skills and Knowledge

Another way to look at jobs is by the skills and knowledge each requires. There are many different ways to identify and list the skills that people draw on to do their jobs. Most jobs require a mix of skills and knowledge, yet the ratio or proportion of the mix depends on the job, the work environment, and the level of support available. For the purpose of setting expectations, jobs can be easily classified as requiring the following skills and knowledge:

1. Technical, scientific, or professional
2. Influencing and managing relationships
3. Organizing and coordinating data and people's efforts
4. Self-management

Most jobs draw on all four areas of skill and knowledge, but in different proportions. For example:

1. Some jobs require a high level of proficiency in a discipline, field, or profession. In such cases, the organization tends to place more weight on people's technical professional proficiency and less on the other areas. Examples are scientists, engineers, and people in the building or construction trades. It's not that they do not have to have customer service, organizational, or self-management skills, but the organization may put less emphasis on these other skill sets.

2. Sales, customer service, counseling, and similar jobs require a greater level of proficiency in relationship management skills (communication, listening, persuading, negotiating, and so on) and the organization tends to place higher value on being proficient in these areas.

3. Managers, general contractors, project managers, logistics, and similar jobs require a greater level of proficiency in skills related to analyzing and organizing data and coordinating people activity.

4. Jobs with little supervision or with a high dependence on self-direction require a greater level of proficiency in self-management, such as

managing one's time, setting priorities, and following through on commitments.

No matter what the emphasis is, you should still measure performance across all areas. If you only concentrate on one area, you risk not getting the performance the organization requires.

Variance or Predictability

A third way to think about jobs is to consider the amount of variance or predictability associated with the job. Some jobs are very routine and predictable; some moderately so; and others very unpredictable. The degree of variance and predictability should lead you to consider measuring people's ability to handle sameness, the very prescribed, the unexpected, and the very ambiguous.

For example, people may not be able to control or predict the amount of work coming in, what others expect, or the consistency of materials or information; however, they are still expected to do the job. Generally, the greater the variance or unpredictability, the higher the level of skills that are required to do the work adequately. Here are some examples:

- Sales representatives (reps) who sell one product or sell to one industry have to deal with less variance than those who sell multiple products or to many industries

- Sales representatives who sell in hostile markets have to be more skilled than those who sell in friendly markets

- Supervisors who direct workers with about the same level of seniority and skill level have less variance than those whose workers consist of new hires and experienced workers or people of widely different ages and ethnic backgrounds

- Managers who lead units with stable labor relations and mature processes have less variance than those who direct units with unstable labor relations or newly evolving processes

- Medical technicians assigned to suburban hospitals have less variance than those who work at inner city trauma centers

Consider using all of these views to help you identify and explain what you will be attending to as you observe and make judgments about your people's performance. Here is a tool you can use to help you select and communicate measures that match your expectations.

TOOL 3.3: HOW TO SELECT MEASURES

Purpose

This set of guidelines is to help you decide what to measure and what measures to use.

How

Together with people who do the job and perhaps someone from human resources:

A. Classify the jobs based on the type of work performed. You might want to use a worksheet similar to one in Figure 3.3. Add as many rows as necessary.

B. In column one, list the jobs

C. In column two, classify the job as piecework, procedural work, process work, mental or intellectual work, or relationship work.

D. Select two to three measures you think are appropriate and put them in column three. Include measures like those listed below and add any that are more appropriate for your situation. Use the worksheet in Figure 3.4 to help you select the measures and what you will accept as evidence of proficiency, productivity, and performance.

E. Discuss what you might use as evidence of someone being productive in column five. Consider:

1. The quantity or volume of work produced

2. The quality of the work produced

3. The timeliness of the work produced

4. The amount of energy consumed to do the work both by the person doing the work and by others, including the boss

5. The impact, both positive and negative, on others who are doing similar or different work, including distractions

6. The cleanup required later, including repairing relationships, work spaces, and equipment

Figure 3.3. Measures Worksheet

1. Job	2. Type	3. Measures	4. Skill Level			5. Evidence	6. Comments
			H	M	L		

Note: H is high level of skills, M is moderate level, and L is low level of skill.

Figure 3.4. Means and Evidence

What Is Important to You?	What Do You Use as Evidence That Your Expectations Are Being Met?
Acceptance	
Accuracy	
Adoption	
Compliance	
Consistency	
Cooperation	
Customer satisfaction	
Cycle time	
Efficient use of resources	
Goal accomplishment	
Meet quota	
Precision	
Predictability	
Quality	
Quantity	
Relationships	
Reliability	
Resource consumption	
Resource costs	
Retention	
Self-reliance	
Teamwork	
Timeliness	

F. Discuss the level of proficiency required of the job and in what combination of skill areas. Note the proficiency level in column four. Assign a percentage or weight across all four skill and knowledge areas:

1. How much of the job requires technical, scientific, or professional knowledge?

2. How much requires self-management skills?

3. How much requires skill in organizing data?

4. How much requires skill in organizing and coordinating human activities?

G. Discuss how much support is available and put that in column six. The more support available, the less skilled people have to be.

1. What support mechanisms are in place to help people perform if they do not have the level of proficiency the job requires?

2. To what degree do people have to work alone versus having some-one always available to answer questions or provide guidance?

3. To what degree are the tasks routine and predictable, and how does that affect the types and levels of skills that are required?

4. To what degree do the tasks that make up the job have well-prescribed procedures?

Hint: Remember, you can measure how work gets done, how much gets done, and the consequences of having done the work.

WHAT TO USE FOR COMPARISON

Not only do you have to decide what to measure, but you have to decide what to use for comparison. Here are some of the typical points of comparison.

History

- How a person performed in the past or what others did in the past
- Past production reports
- Past customer survey data
- Past internal audit or regulatory reports

Other People

- How an individual or a group compares to others who do similar work under similar conditions

Standards

- How a product, procedure, or process compares to an industry standard

Expected Results

- How actual results compare to the assumptions about what the results should have been

Aftereffects

- What the impact was on co-workers, customers, costs, resource consumption, and relationships compared to what happened in the past or to what was planned to occur

TIPS

Here are some suggestions to help you communicate and reinforce your expectations:

1. Do your homework. Find out what is in people's job descriptions. If what you expect is different from what is in a job description, either change it or change your expectations.

2. Confirm that your understanding of what is expected of you and your group is the same as others' understanding.

3. In collaboration with your people and any others you believe bring a legitimate perspective, define the deliverables for your work unit and the teams and individuals in it.

4. Identify what you use as evidence of proficiency and productivity.

5. Always have more than one set of measures, for example:

   • Sales volume + cost of sales + cost to service the sale

   • Customer satisfaction + cost of service + use of other resources

6. Create a picture of where your unit falls in the organization's larger process of producing goods and services to the marketplace.

SUMMARY

Someone has to set expectations and decide what measures to use to judge whether or not those expectations were met. Measures are the criteria used to determine whether you are ahead or behind. The challenge is how to select measures that support the results you want and make sure in the process you don't accidentally encourage behaviors that are not in the best interest of the organization. Alignment starts with being clear and in agreement on the objectives and deliverables of the job. Once this is clear you can begin to identify attributes that would indicate that the objectives are being accomplished in ways that are in keeping with the organization's goals and values.

Just as you take cues from top management as to what is important, your people do the same with you. They interpret what is important to you by the questions you ask, what you talk about, what you report to others, and what you measure. Therefore, it is important to be clear in your own mind about what you expect and what you will use as evidence of performance.

WHERE TO LEARN MORE

Here are some suggestions about where to learn more about measuring.

Hale, J. *Performance-Based Certification* (San Francisco, CA: Jossey-Bass, 2002).

Hale, J. *Performance-Based Evaluation* (San Francisco, CA: Jossey-Bass, 2002).

NOTE

1. The definitions for occupation, job, duty, and task were adapted from those in E. J. McCormick, *Job Analysis: Methods and Application* (New York: AMACOM, 1979). Other references for better understanding occupations, jobs, and tasks are *Handbook for Analyzing Jobs* (Washington, DC: U.S. Department of Labor, Manpower Administration [Stock No. 2900–0131], 1972) and W. H. Melching and S.D. Borcher, *Procedures for Constructing and Using Task Inventories* (Columbus, OH: Center for Vocational and Technical Education [Research and Development Series No. 91], The Ohio State University, 1973).

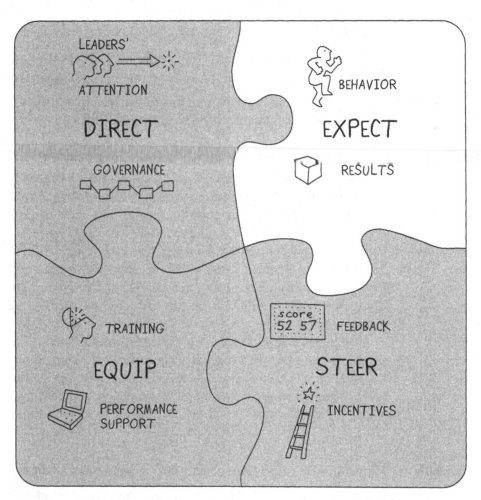

Figure 4.1. Leadership Roles

Lynn Kearny, CPT, Graphic Recorder

Chapter 4

How to Identify Behaviors That Lead to Performance

So what does good enough look like?

*T*he first part of setting expectations is letting people know on what basis their performance will be judged, what the measures will be. The second part is being able to explain the behaviors you want because you believe them to be critical for performance. This chapter is about the behaviors and activities that are essential for performance. Specifically, it is about the importance of taking the time to identify the behaviors you want and do not want so you are in a better position to provide coaching and feedback.

The need to better understand the role of behaviors in achieving performance is one of the reasons why organizations are investing in the development of competencies. *Competencies* are statements that describe the behaviors or attributes organizations want in their employees on the assumption that these characteristics correlate with results. *Core competencies* are the characteristics that organizations want everyone to exhibit, as they believe they are appropriate for all job levels and all functions. *Technical and professional competencies* are unique to jobs or job roles.

The word "competency" usually refers to the label or name of a family of skills, such as leadership or innovation. The expression "competency statement" usually refers to the description of behaviors that give evidence of the skill. Depending on the level of detail in the descriptions, competency statements can communicate what is expected as well as help you give feedback and coach new behaviors.

PERFORMANCE IMPROVEMENT

From a performance improvement perspective, people require and deserve to know what is expected of them. They deserve to understand that their performance is partially based on their behaviors and partially on their accomplishments. Performance measures help because they define accomplishment. Competency statements describe the behaviors the organization values because it believes those behaviors contribute to people's productivity. This chapter is about how to identify the desired and undesired behaviors and use them to communicate expectations.

COMMON MISSTEPS

Here are some of the mistakes managers and supervisors make related to behaviors and competencies:

1. They avoid asking HR to help identify key behaviors or link the competencies they do have to tasks or job roles.

2. They do not bother to question the circumstances that made one set of behaviors effective sometimes, but ineffective if the situation changes.

3. They fail to understand competencies and how they can be used.

4. They think competencies are HR's responsibility and do not want to become involved.

5. They fail to exercise their rights as consumers of HR's services and do not insist that any competencies developed be user-friendly and useful.

6. They overlook the opportunity to use competencies to help them better articulate what they expect and how they judge others' performance.

COMPETENCIES AND COMPETENCY STATEMENTS

Competency statements have different levels of detail, and some statements are not sufficiently specific to help anyone identify appropriate and inappropriate behaviors. For example:

- Labels—single words or short phrases, such as leadership, interpersonal skills, and problem solving. Labels and simple statements have no meaning to individuals and are difficult to connect to the day-to-day tasks. Perhaps worse is that everyone talks as if they understand and agree, yet if you were to question them you would discover that each has a different interpretation of the skill being discussed.

- Brief descriptions—short paragraphs that may describe what it is and why it is important. An example is leadership: "The person provides consistent direction and support so others stay focused on what is important." But this description is still very generic and does not explain how leadership is demonstrated in different jobs or at different job levels.

Figure 4.2. Comparison of Leader Behaviors

Problem Solve—Obtain sufficient data to analyze a situation and draw conclusions from which you can develop a plan of action or provide an answer		
Needs Development	**Meets Expectations**	**Exceeds Expectations**
The person:	The person:	The person:
Misses the point	Probes for what is relevant	Begins to grasp the complexities
Fails to seek information	Confirms the accuracy of the information	Knows when critical information is missing
Fails to confirm the accuracy of information	Has enough information to understand the point	Points out discrepancies in data
States opinion without the facts	Summarizes and interprets the data	Suggests solutions or actions based on the data

Other competency statements have more detail, for example:

• They may include examples of behaviors that illustrate the competency. An example is under the "meets expectations" column in Figure 4.2.

• They may include examples of behaviors that indicate a person needs development and exceeds expectations (see all three columns in Figure 4.2).

Finally, some competency statements go so far as to show how the behaviors differ based on the job level, as shown in Figure 4.3.

When competency statements include examples of appropriate and inappropriate behaviors, they (1) help communicate what is expected; (2) give managers language to model when describing the behaviors they want to see more of or less of; and (3) allow employees to monitor their own behavior. Competency statements can be very helpful in suggesting language that describes behaviors in ways that allow people to better understand what they should do differently or what they are doing right. Competency statements, however, are rarely linked to tasks or jobs, or do not address results and, therefore, should not be used alone when giving feedback. Goals are what people plan to do, and results are what happens. Competencies are the skills, knowledge, and effort that caused the results to happen. For example, a project took longer than what was planned, adding unnecessary costs. The project manager blamed the cost overruns on others for not cooperating and changes in the scope of the project. These may have contributed to the problem to some extent; however, the manager should be able to describe how the project manager's weaknesses, perhaps in negotiation or contingency planning, also contributed to the problem.

Figure 4.3. Behaviors Across Roles

Problem Solve—Obtain sufficient data to analyze a situation and draw conclusions from which you can develop a plan of action or provide an answer				
Individual Contributor	**Supervisor**	**Manager**	**Mid-Level Manager**	**Senior Manager**
The person: Probes for what is relevant Confirms the accuracy of the information Has enough information to understand the point Summarizes and interprets the data	The person: Gets to what is relevant Has enough information to understand the issues Considers one or more alternatives Appropriately times the recommendation or decision	The person: Provides expert advice Develops proposals or recommendations to address complex issues of a strategic nature Interprets policy	The person: Assures that critical information was considered Assures that information used in the analysis was valid Assures two or more viable alternatives were considered Considers the impact on other divisions	The person: Develops effective long-term strategies to solve complex problems Serves as point of appeal to resolve internal disputes

At the end of this chapter is a comprehensive job aid that suggests behaviors for five jobs at the "needs development," "effective," and "highly effective" levels for twelve competencies. You can modify the job levels, the competencies, and the behaviors to meet your own requirements. The intent is to help you better describe what you expect to see on the job, compared with what you do see. The job aid will also help you in discussions with staff about what behaviors are appropriate, given the level of the job, the other support systems that are available, and the results that are expected.

If you have competencies already developed by your organization, take the time to read them. Ask yourself:

• What assumptions were made that make these statements relevant to my work, my people's work, and what we are expected to accomplish?

• How do they show up in my work and in my people's work?

• How can we use them to monitor our own behaviors?

• How can they help me give people better, more constructive feedback?

• What do people require to demonstrate the desired behaviors—role models, training, coaching, or reinforcement?

Once you understand the competencies, you are in a better position to link them to the jobs your people do.

TOOL 4.1: HOW TO IDENTIFY DESIRED BEHAVIORS

Purpose

This set of guidelines is meant to help you identify the behaviors you want of your people. You can use it whether you have competency statements or not. It can be used to identify behaviors specific to a task or to work behaviors in general.

How

Preferably, work with someone from training or human resources and the people who do the task well. If you can, have someone join you who depends on the task being done well, such as an internal customer.

A. Identify the task or job you want to work on.

B. List the activities that make up the task or job. Consider outlining or mapping the steps used to do the task if it involves a process. Record everyone's answers on a flip chart so they can see the whole list.

C. Ask everyone to list what a person must know to do the task well. Record everyone's answers on a flip chart.

D. Ask them to think of a person who does the job very well. Then ask them to recall a time when the person did a task well. Next, ask what that person did specifically that made him or her stand out? Record everyone's answers.

E. Ask them to think of a person who disappointed them. Then ask them to recall a time when the person failed to live up to their expectations. Next, ask what that person did specifically that made him or her fall short of expectations. Record everyone's answers.

F. Divide the two lists from D and E into two groups: (1) those behaviors that are specific to the task and (2) those that reflect general work behaviors such as ethics, initiative, or other areas. General behaviors are best dealt with during the hiring process, whereas people can usually be trained to do the task-specific behaviors.

G. Use the information to come up with a list of behaviors that good performers exhibit on a regular basis. They can be the behaviors you want to see because they are required by law, are necessary to do the job appropriately, are in keeping with the organization's values, or what

Figure 4.4. Performance Checklist Template

Name of Task:	Step or Attribute	✓ if OK	Comments

customers expect. It is important that people who do the job know the expected behaviors. It also helps if they know what is unacceptable so they can make better decisions about how to behave in unusually difficult situations.

H. Ask training to help you create performance checklists that your people can use to coach each other and monitor their own performance and that you can use to reinforce the desired behaviors. See Figure 4.4 for a template you can use. Here are some hints to get you started.

1. If the task involves a procedure (for example, update customers records online):

   a. List the steps that make up the procedure

   b. Note which steps must be done

   c. Indicate where a sequence must be followed

2. If the task involves judgment or is less procedural (prepare the capital budget):

   a. List the attributes, criteria, factors, or accomplishments that must be there

   b. Strive for a level of detail that is useful and unambiguous (less experienced employees require more detail)

   c. Mark those attributes, criteria, factors, or accomplishment that must be present

Hint: Locate and make use of industry or job standards. Someone may already have defined what constitutes good performance. Check out the standards developed by the State of Illinois, for example, as they are written at a sufficient level of detail to permit assessing someone's performance. They are free.[1]

**USING
COMPETENCIES
TO SELECT PEOPLE**

Competencies or a list of behaviors and activities can be used to help you find people with the skills and abilities you want. Specifically, they can help you develop questions to ask during the selection and hiring phase. Competencies are especially useful for creating questions that uncover how people think, set priorities, handle adversity, and work with others. You simply ask people to describe what they did, how they handled a situation, and why. However, you also identify ahead of time the information you want revealed by the answer. For example, if you asked someone to describe how he or she handled a budget cut, the loss of a key person, or a major change in direction, you want to compare the answers to some criteria. If you do not know what you are listening for, you risk hearing a lot of interesting stories but with no basis for comparison. You could end up comparing people on their ability to tell stories or on the uniqueness of the story, rather than on whether they have the attributes you think are important for your work. Here is a set of guidelines you can use to develop questions designed to uncover how people handle situations, deal with problems, and manage relationships.

TOOL 4.2: HOW TO DEVELOP BEHAVIORAL INTERVIEW QUESTIONS

Purpose

This set of guidelines is meant to help you create questions to determine whether people possess the competencies or abilities you require.

How

Preferably work with someone from training or HR and members of your staff.

  A. Identify the competencies or abilities most critical to the job you want to fill or the task you want to assign.

  B. Create an opening or lead-in statement, such as:

   1. "Tell me about a time when you [were asked to do X, found out that X changed, had X happen]. What did you do? How did you handle it? Why?"

   2. "Here is the situation we have here [lost a key person, have two people refusing to cooperate, have an unhappy customer ready to leave us]. How do you think we should handle it? Why?"

   3. "Here is a situation we found ourselves in last year [describe the situation]. What would you have done in a similar situation? Why?"

  C. Before you interview anyone, list the information that you will listen for because it might indicate the person has the ability to do what you require. Consider things such as:

1. Took the time to tell people, kept others informed
2. Checked out the information to be sure it was accurate
3. Put together a plan
4. Involved others to obtain their input, support, or advice
5. Identified the implications (on budget, timeline, other promises, and so on)
6. Took the initiative to learn more, explain the ramifications, and so forth
7. Talked to the people directly
8. Explained the consequences if the behavior continued
9. Documented the event
10. Checked with the appropriate people to confirm what to do

D. Use a different lead-in statement to find out whether the person's first set of answers is similar to the second set. You want corroborating evidence.

E. List the same information you are listening for as you did for the first question.

F. Repeat the process to confirm the presence of other competencies or abilities.

G. Corroborate what you learn from the person's application or resume and references.

Hint: Ask someone else to listen in on the interview and use the same criteria to judge the applicant's ability while you do the same. Once the interview is over, compare your answers. Discuss any differences of opinion.

TEAM MEMBER SKILLS FOR TECHNOLOGY

Teri is an information systems implementation manager. She has numerous teams reporting to her. The teams were set up to develop different aspects of the new computer system, including database design, user interface design, reporting requirements, and training users. The organization was prepared to detail people to the teams for up to eighteen months. To help her select the best combination of team members and team leaders, Teri first identified the technical skills required of all of the team members. Next, she identified the project planning and management skills required of the team leaders. The list of skills she came up with for the team leader for project management is shown in Figure 4.5.

Figure 4.5. Sample Form to Interview for Project Management Skills

Project Management Skills	The skills required for keeping all resources on track to ensure optimal success during implementation and ongoing use
Critical Skill Category	Evidence of Skills
Project Management	Is able to provide direction to individuals or a team using project management principles, tools, and methodologies
Goal Identification	Creates a project plan and budget that identifies milestones and assigns responsibilities; identifies achievable goals based on strategic plans; meets the performance predicted by the plan
Results and Status Communication	Communicates project results; creates and distributes project status reports
Project Communication	Manages the interpersonal aspects of project planning and management; maintains positive relationships with individuals and groups involved in projects
Time/Budget/Resource Management	Delivers projects on time, meeting specifications, scope, and budget
Resource Identification and Negotiation	Facilitates and gains agreement to project resources, costs, time lines, and outputs
Contingency Planning	Identifies risks and contingency plans; controls project issues; and manages changes as they arise
Project Management Measurement	Evaluates the effectiveness of his or her project management practices using agreed-on effectiveness measures; uses this information to improve his or her project management and to plan for future projects or changes/improvements needed for project management tools
Managing Change	Is able to manage change systematically and flexibly, whether the change is within or outside of one's control; can cope effectively with change and is able to handle risk and uncertainty effectively; makes decisions and takes action as needed to get the job done
People Management	Is able to direct the activities, performance, and attitudes of individuals and groups to effectively pursue agreed-on work goals and objectives

Note: The example was created by Teri Lund and her partner, Susan Barksdale, of Strategic Assessment and Evaluation Associates. They can be reached at tlund_bls@MSN.com.

She used the list of skills and activities to develop job descriptions, to communicate expectations, and to create interview questions. Here are two of the interview questions she used to help her select the team leader:

1. Tell me about a time when you were expected to communicate project results. How did you do that? How were the results used and by whom?

    Here is what she listened for in the candidate's response: Had a reason for communicating results; knew why it was being done; knew how the results were used; made sure the communication was made, effective, and reached the people as intended.

2. Tell me about a time when there was major change made to a project that affected you. What did you do? How did you handle it?

    Here is what she listened for in the candidate's response: Put together a plan to determine the impact of the change; determined the impact of the change on staffing, budget, promises to client, deadlines; communicated the change to team members; let the client know of the implications of the change on schedule or budget.

Once the team was in place, she again used the list of behaviors to help develop team-member skills. Teri and the employee discussed each activity. Teri asked the employee to rate how well he or she was at doing each one. She would then share her observations, and together they would come up with a plan for improving. The plan included what Teri would do and what the employee would do.

TIPS

Here are some suggestions to help you align behaviors to performance measures and the organization's goals.

1. Take the time to understand the competencies developed by your organization.
2. Ask human resources to help you relate the competencies to your people's jobs and performance expectations.
3. If the competencies lack sufficient detail to be useful, ask human resources to help you add the appropriate level of detail.
4. Involve your own people in identifying the behaviors you want.

SUMMARY

Sometimes organizational goals are too removed from people's day-to-day activities or responsibilities. This can also be true of competency statements if they are too lofty or too abstract to be meaningful. It may be hard to argue over statements like "assesses risk," yet it does not tell you how the competency shows up in different jobs or under different circumstances. A lot of people would prefer clear directions for every circumstance, but this is not possible, as many jobs come with some degree of judgment. Competency statements and behavioral descriptions can help explain what is expected and under what circumstances.

Competency statements can help you be more aware of the behaviors that lead to performance so that you can explain their importance. Competency statements can help you select job candidates and develop your people. Whether your organization has competency statements or not, there are things you can do to identify the behaviors that are essential for effective performance. For example, you can talk to

- Those who are good at doing a task
- Those who are the customers of those who are expected to do a task
- Those whose work is affected the most when a task is or is not done well

If you do not have competency statements or descriptions of desired behaviors, ask training or human resources to help you develop them.

WHERE TO LEARN MORE

Here are some books that can help you better understand competencies and how they are used.

Kravetz, D.J. *The Directory for Building Competencies.* (Bartlett, IL: Kravetz Associates, 1995). An excellent paperback full of clearly written examples of many of the more troublesome skill sets, including interpersonal skills, verbal skills, listening, planning, organizing, and more. There are thirty-one competency areas.

Lombardo, M., and Eichinger, B. *FYI: For Your Improvement* (3rd ed.) (Minneapolis, MN: Lominger, 2002). Check the web page at www.lominger.com.

NOTE

1. The Illinois Occupational Skills Standards and Credentialing Council established teams made up of industry representatives, academics, and workers to develop standards. The Council has endorsed over forty-eight projects addressing more than two hundred occupations. The standards are free. For the most recent list go to www.standards.siu.edu.

TOOL 4.3: JOB AID FOR DESCRIBING BEHAVIORS BY JOB LEVEL AND THE LEVEL OF PERFORMANCE

Purpose

This job aid is designed so that you can modify it to make it specific enough to help you identify the behaviors to focus on and talk about with employees.

Design

The job aid is in five tables. Each describes behaviors at the "needs development," "effective," and "highly effective" levels for one job category across twelve competencies. The twelve competencies include:

1. Problem Solve—obtain sufficient data to analyze a situation and draw conclusions from which you can develop a plan of action or provide an answer.

2. Create—spot things that need to be changed, recognize where improvement will help, and conceive of new ideas or programs to meet organizational needs.

3. Plan—identify and describe the activities, resources, and timeline necessary to accomplish a goal.

4. Implement—carry out the activities required to accomplish a goal.

5. Advise—give advice to help resolve individual and organization issues.

6. Communicate—inform others of your observations, requirements, and expectations using multiple media and channels.

7. Build and Use Relationships—establish trust and mutual respect that results in productive relationships.

8. Lead—provide consistent direction and support so that others stay focused on what is important.

9. Cooperate—collaborate with others in ways that accomplish goals and lead to meaningful results.

10. Develop Self and Others—learn and help others learn.

11. Think and Act Strategically—identify pressures and their implications on a specific course of action and ways to circumvent them.

12. Think and Act Globally—identify and weigh factors that might contribute to or interfere with success and the implications of your actions on others.

Modify the list of competencies and the sample behaviors to better reflect your situation.

How to Use the Job Aids

A. Read over the competencies and select those that are relevant to you.

B. Select one of the job categories and read the behaviors under it.

C. Using the model as an example, identify the behaviors you want to see in your people. Add to or modify the behaviors as necessary.

D. Identify the behaviors you believe support accuracy, adoption and acceptance of new ideas, goal accomplishment, quality, quantity, compliance, and timeliness.

E. The model suggests a rating scale of 1 (needs development), 2 (effective), and 3 (highly effective). You can choose to eliminate the scale or modify it to fit your situation.

F. Share your observations about the competencies and behaviors with your people. Together discuss the behaviors and why you think they are important to performance.

G. Together decide on how you and your people will use this information to monitor performance.

Hint: Think of people who are high in a competency. Think of people who are not. Use those examples to help you initially describe what you do and do not want to see in others' behaviors.

TOOL 4.3A: JOB AID FOR DESCRIBING BEHAVIORS BY JOB LEVEL AND LEVEL OF PERFORMANCE—SENIOR MANAGER

Competencies	Senior Manager			Your Rating:			Your Rationale
	Needs Development 1	Effective 2	Highly Effective 3	1	2	3	
Problem Solve—obtain sufficient data to analyze a situation and draw conclusions from which you can develop a plan of action or provide an answer	Fails to develop or provide a strategy that others can use to direct their efforts	Develops effective long-term strategies / Serves as point of appeal to resolve internal disputes	Supports and coaches others to improve at strategic planning, critical thinking, and problem solving				
Create—spot things that need to be changed, recognize where improvement will help, and conceive of new ideas or programs to meet organizational needs	Is late in putting teams or systems in place to deal with the organizational issues / Only responds to requests to enhance the work environment	Sponsors teams and projects to develop innovative information and development systems / Supports the development of policies and practices that enhance the work environment	Sponsors groups who develop models and systems to forecast organizational needs and test new ideas related to enhancing the work environment and its ability to attract and retain high performers				
Plan—identify and describe the activities, resources, and timeline necessary to accomplish a goal	Fails to involve staff or appoint staff to develop long-term staffing plans / Challenges staff's budgets without providing guidance on how to improve them	Works through staff to develop company/unit staffing plans and forecasts / Approves budgets and headcounts / Defines long-term needs	Sponsors the development of forecasting models and alternative staffing arrangements / Challenges budgets and headcount while coaching staff in how to develop ones that meet business needs				

Behavior				
Implement—carry out the activities required to accomplish a goal	Drops sponsorship of programs, leaving them to flounder and not fully live up to expectations	Assures policies are translated into operational terms and are implemented; Allocates sufficient resources for the function to meet its goals	Works with staff and stakeholders to assure programs are fully operational and institutionalized; Works with staff to develop innovative models for getting and using resources	
Advise—give advice to help resolve individual and organization issues	Advice is simplistic and fails to develop senior management's ability to grasp issues	Initiates and sustains effective relationships with senior management; Provides expert advice	Enhances senior management's appreciation and understanding of issues; Invites the use of outside expertise when appropriate	
Communicate—informs others of observations, requirements, and expectations using multiple media and channels	Avoids opportunities to facilitate debate or present complex issues so that management can make better decisions; Discourages staff from initiating serious discourse related to issues	Assures processes and systems are in place to support internal communication and coordination; Keeps up-to-date on trends, issues, and new developments; Represents the organization to outside agencies	Encourages staff to seek and create opportunities to represent and present new ideas related to issues; Takes the lead to assure voice is heard and is up-to-date on business issues; Continually communicates vision	

(Continued)

TOOL 4.3A: JOB AID FOR DESCRIBING BEHAVIORS BY JOB LEVEL AND LEVEL OF PERFORMANCE—SENIOR MANAGER (Continued)

Competencies	Senior Manager			Your Rating:			Your Rationale
	Needs Development 1	Effective 2	Highly Effective 3	1	2	3	
Build and Use Relationships—establish trust and mutual respect that result in productive relationships	Is ineffective at using relationships to assure people or self receives a fair hearing when either presents difficult issues or an unpopular position	Leverages relationships to champion innovative programs Receives a fair hearing for own and others' ideas and concerns	Is able to cultivate new relationships to assure wider support for new ideas Links own agendas with those of the business Acts as a confidential advisor, yet uses the information to solve problems				
Lead—provide consistent direction and support so others stay focused on what is important	Metrics and outcomes are not well-defined Does not take the time to assure staff understand goals and objectives, particularly those that appear in conflict or compete for resources	Assures programs have metrics and defined outcomes Sets goals Assures staff understands their goals and objectives Provides direction to multiple functions in ways that help them set priorities and develop their own plans Links metrics and outcomes to those of the business Steps up to being accountable for effectiveness	Fosters innovative solutions to working with limited resources and conflicting objectives Balances goals and timetables to achieve the most from staff Spots under- or over-engineered plans and solutions and seeks to modify them for practical application				

Cooperate—collaborate with others in ways that accomplish goals and lead to meaningful results	Lack of direction fosters strife among staff instead of collaboration and innovation. When serves as a team leader, the teams are ineffective and experience internal strife	When serves as team leader or player, teams are effective and accomplish their goals, and participants feel their time was well spent. Balances own staff's workload with demands from other departments	Rewards innovation and collaboration. Reminds teams of the synergy that is possible through teamwork. Fosters an environment that encourages collaboration, not competition
Develop Self and Others—learn and help others learn	Assumes needs little or no development and is positioned to respond to new challenges. Fails to participate in self-development or company sponsored training	Determines whether new approaches are needed for emerging issues and, if so, whether needs development to come up with those new approaches. Participates in self-development and company-sponsored training. Mentors others	Rewards development and assures resources are available to support it. Insists the business benefit from development. Shows support for and participates actively in self-development and company-sponsored training
Think and Act Strategically—identify pressures and their implications on a specific course of action and ways to circumvent them	Assumes policies support corporate policies. Discourages internal examination of policies	Evaluates program measures and impact. Assures policies are developed that support corporate goals	Fosters internal debate to assure policies and practices support the business

(Continued)

TOOL 4.3A: JOB AID FOR DESCRIBING BEHAVIORS BY JOB LEVEL AND LEVEL OF PERFORMANCE—SENIOR MANAGER (Continued)

| Competencies | Senior Manager | | | Your Rating: | | | Your Rationale |
	Needs Development 1	Effective 2	Highly Effective 3	1	2	3	
		Challenges outmoded practices and fosters continuous improvement	Avoids management gimmicks, superficial trends, or fads that waste time and staff				
Think and Act Globally—identify and weigh factors that might contribute to or interfere with success and the implications of your actions on others	Does not foster critical examination of practices or policies in terms of how they impact the business in different parts of the world	Responds to organizational effectiveness issues at a global level Works with staff to identify and weigh the consequences of actions that inadvertently set precedent and possibly undermine the business' objectives in different parts of the world	Anticipates the need for different policies and practices in order to support the business in different parts of the world Recognizes hidden impacts and addresses them proactively				

TOOL 4.3B: JOB AID FOR DESCRIBING BEHAVIORS BY JOB LEVEL AND LEVEL OF PERFORMANCE—MID-LEVEL MANAGER

| Competencies | Mid-Level Manager | | | Your Rating: | | | Your Rationale |
	Needs Development 1	Effective 2	Highly Effective 3	1	2	3	
Problem Solve—obtain sufficient data to analyze a situation and draw conclusions from which you can develop a plan of action or provide an answer	Accepts information on face value Fails to challenge staff's thinking or processes Fails to require staff to validate their assumptions or conclusions Only considers the immediate impact	Assures critical information was considered Assures information used in the analysis was valid Assures two or more viable alternatives were considered Considers the impact on other divisions	Models critical thinking skills consistently Coaches or rehearses staff's presentations to management in terms of their logic and processes Asks questions in ways that allow staff to think through issues and implications				
Create—spot things that need to be changed, recognize where improvement will help, and conceive of new ideas or programs to meet organizational needs	Fails to insist that requirements be based on multiple perspectives Fails to require prototypes, pilots, or user acceptance studies on major programmatic changes	Facilitates the development of the requirements Assures proposed designs meet the specifications Seeks ways for proposed designs to be sufficiently flexible and have alternative uses	Challenges others' thinking about the requirements in terms of time span, long-term costs and value, hidden side effects, and so forth				
Plan—identify and describe the activities, resources, and timeline necessary to accomplish a goal	Fails to challenge plans' viability in terms of their timelines or resource requirements	Recognizes when plans and timelines are and are not viable or lack sufficient resources	Coaches how to build more viable plans and handle resource contingencies				

(Continued)

TOOL 4.3B: JOB AID FOR DESCRIBING BEHAVIORS BY JOB LEVEL AND LEVEL OF PERFORMANCE—MID-LEVEL MANAGER (Continued)

Competencies	Mid-Level Manager			Your Rating:			Your Rationale
	Needs Development 1	Effective 2	Highly Effective 3	1	2	3	
Implement—carry out the activities required to accomplish a goal	Misses opportunities to leverage other investments and resources	Sees opportunities to leverage other investments and resources to optimize a plan's benefits without sacrificing the original objectives of the plan	Acts on opportunities to leverage other investments and resources Able to compromise without sacrificing the objectives of the original plan				
	Reacts to barriers Initiates relationships only after they have become a barrier Fails to give adequate time or thought to the job of spokesperson or champion	Anticipates barriers Leverages relationships to remove barriers Supports by being a spokesperson Is a champion of initiatives	Forecasts the impact of other initiatives in terms of how they might compete for resources, be perceived as contradictory, or distract stakeholders and proposes tactics to eliminate, leverage, or mitigate them				
Advise—give advice to help resolve individual and organization issues	Misses opportunities to coach or advise management Advice is questioned or not supported by other experts Fails to stay up-to-date on industry trends or legal issues	Coaches senior management on sensitive relationship and image issues Provides expert testimony when required Monitors industry and legal trends	Initiates opportunities to discreetly coach and advise senior management Effectively represents management in internal and external meetings Influences industry practices and legal decisions				

Communicate—inform others of observations, requirements, and expectations using multiple media and channels	Becomes so enamored with the complexity of the message, fails to focus people's attention on what really matters	Delivers briefings that quickly and accurately convey status or need for action on complex issues Delivers persuasive arguments that help management make more informed decisions Leverages the available channels and media	Coaches staff in how to make more effective briefings, presentations, use of media and channels Points out the critical issues, culls out the noise, so that management stays focused on what matters
Build and Use Relationships—establish trust and mutual respect that results in productive relationships	Acts as a fair-weather friend Aligns self with groups or individuals with personal versus business agendas	Establishes relationships with key opinion leaders Seeks to understand opposing opinions to assure they are accurately represented Builds strategies to influence others in ways that are face-saving, legitimizes their opinions, and builds a mutually respectful relationship	Remains politically neutral without sacrificing own position or ideas or being seen as a non-player Sustains the respect of people with very different opinions or who risk loss of status when difficult decisions are made

(Continued)

TOOL 4.3B: JOB AID FOR DESCRIBING BEHAVIORS BY JOB LEVEL AND LEVEL OF PERFORMANCE—MID-LEVEL MANAGER (Continued)

Competencies	Mid-Level Manager			Your Rating:			Your Rationale
	Needs Development 1	Effective 2	Highly Effective 3	1	2	3	
Lead—provide consistent direction and support so others stay focused on what is important	Exerts no opinion or position on key issues, sits on the fence until knows whose opinion will prevail Does not take the initiative to seek out opposing views and understand them Overly simplifies or discounts minority opinions	Advises leaders on how to influence others Enrolls others, gains their support for major initiatives Continually polls to assure people's support, proactively surfaces opposition, and assures opposing opinions are accurately represented	Helps shape other leaders' positions on key issues Effective at getting people to support initiatives earlier or faster Takes a position on key issues, does not waffle, yet is well-informed of the opposing opinions				
Cooperate—collaborate with others in ways that accomplish goals and lead to meaningful results	Fails to anticipate or recognize teams' need for intervention or coaching Only participates on teams when required to do so Seeks to appease rather than help teamwork constructively	Identifies the need for teams Provides support for teams Participates on strategic teams by facilitating constructive debate to assure diverse opinions are heard Acknowledges how others contributed to own ability to contribute	Models effective team playing and leadership by participating on teams and contributing to their success Monitors teams' progress and provides coaching as needed				

Develop Self and Others—learn and help others learn	Lacks personal development plans Does not seek opportunities to compare self with what others are doing Does not coach unless asked to do so	Monitors own development based on feedback, organizational needs, and professional goals Actively coaches others	Serves as a benchmark for others Acts on opportunities to develop others Rewards those who serve as coaches or mentors to others
Think and Act Strategically—identify pressures and their implications on a specific course of action and ways to circumvent them	Fails to track or consider trends Monitors activities rather than accomplishments	Actively polls or checks the pulse of key stakeholders Insists on regular, frequent status updates in terms of goal accomplishment Initiates fresh ideas on how to achieve the organization's long-term goals	Puts systems in place to track internal and external events and trends Monitors how well the organization is meeting its goals in light of new developments Supports the exploration of fresh ideas
Think and Act Globally—identify and weigh factors that might contribute to or interfere with success and the implications of actions on others	Fails to consider multiple variables when evaluating recommendations Fails to consider the longer-term consequences of actions or decisions	Weighs risk on multiple factors such as cost, image, relationship, impact on other initiatives, and so forth Seeks or supports the development of models, scenarios that approximate probable consequences or emulate alternative futures	Models critical thinking by making explicit what was considered, how variables were weighed, and how final recommendation or position was derived Rewards and encourages staff who seek to improve their risk assessment models and processes

TOOL 4.3C: JOB AID FOR DESCRIBING BEHAVIORS BY JOB LEVEL AND LEVEL OF PERFORMANCE—FIRST-LEVEL MANAGER

Competencies	First-Level Manager			Your Rating:			Your Rationale
	Needs Development 1	Effective 2	Highly Effective 3	1	2	3	
Problem Solve—obtain sufficient data to analyze a situation and draw conclusions from which you can develop a plan of action or provide an answer	Advice is dated Proposals and recommendations fail to reflect the complexity or the strategic issues Avoids interpreting policy	Provides expert advice Develops proposals or recommendations to address complex issues of a strategic nature Interprets policy	Advice is forward-thinking and visionary Proposals and recommendations compare alternatives and consider risk Interpretations consider potential precedent setting and being in conflict with other policies				
Create—spot things that need to be changed, recognize where improvement will help, and conceive of new ideas or programs to meet organizational needs	Designs are simplistic or rigid Fails to recognize where specifications and requirements do not match	Develops complex designs and modifications that meet requirements and are flexible and versatile	Develops business cases that value the cost of flexibility and versatility compared to the cost of utility and timeliness				
Plan—identify and describe the activities, resources, and timeline necessary to accomplish a goal	Sees no need to coordinate with other units Fails to see the impact of plans on others' resources	Involves staff in designing plans and building models that identify the impact on other units or divisions	Builds complex plans that span one or more years and require coordination across units and divisions				

Behavior			
Implement—carry out the activities required to accomplish a goal	Has to rely on others to help obtain the required resources Misses opportunities to engage other stakeholders in implementation	Secures resources that will benefit from any plan or change Builds teams to support implementation	Looks to leverage other investments, resources Gets others to share the costs and risks and assume long-term ownership of a program, product, or system Uses implementation teams as opportunities to build strategic relationships and identify barriers
Advise—give advice to help resolve individual and organization issues	Advice fails to consider the impact on other functions or divisions Does not leverage opportunities to enroll other groups Technical advice is shortsighted or out-of-date	Advises others on how to develop and implement changes with minimal disruption or impact on relations Facilitates cross-divisional groups Provides technical expertise to training	Uses requests for advice as opportunities to build relationships, identify barriers, aid implementation, surface issues, and gain buy-in for other initiatives
Communicate—informs others of observations, requirements, and expectations using multiple media and channels	Has trouble managing a group in training Becomes sidetracked with stories Focuses attention on self instead of the objective	Trains managers and employees Gives presentations to employees and outside groups Presents the position of special interests	Uses case studies and scenarios to gain learner participation Develops innovative ways to explain complex ideas Helps others to see the implications and complexities

(Continued)

TOOL 4.3C: JOB AID FOR DESCRIBING BEHAVIORS BY JOB LEVEL AND LEVEL OF PERFORMANCE—FIRST-LEVEL MANAGER (Continued)

Competencies	First-Level Manager			Your Rating:			Your Rationale
	Needs Development 1	Effective 2	Highly Effective 3	1	2	3	
Build and Use Relationships—establish trust and mutual respect that result in productive relationships	Is unable to establish relations across levels or functions Is uninformed of management's feelings or positions	Has effective relations with people at different levels, in different functions, uses those relations to stay informed and resolve conflicts	Uses relationships and network to facilitate solving problems, gain cooperation, and mitigate hurt feelings				
Lead—provide consistent direction and support so others stay focused on what is important	Fails to see the need for change or new programs Polarizes people's opinions versus getting them to compromise	Sees the need for programs Finds funds and support for programs and implements them Mentors others in providing leadership	Anticipates the need for organizational change, enrolls others in the vision, gains their commitment to support the change				
Cooperate—collaborate with others in ways that accomplish goals and leads to meaningful results	Fails to communicate new developments or decisions to staff and peers Fails to poll teams as to their needs Is an ineffective team leader	Makes sure programs are communicated to staff Polls teams to learn their needs Is an effective team leader	Engenders a sense of camaraderie and community among staff Works to establish an identity by branding programs				

Develop Self and Others—learn and help others learn	Does not support own or staff's development through professional associations or other means	Polls customers and monitors program impact and uses the information to identify developmental needs	Negotiates for development funds Creates developmental opportunities for self and staff
Think and Act Strategically—identify pressures and their implications on a specific course of action and ways to circumvent them	Fails to consider long-term implications, either positive or negative Tracks activity not impact or goal achievement	Measures the effectiveness of programs, how they were implemented, and their effect on others Supports continuous improvement	Develops innovative ways to measure impact and customer satisfaction Identifies ways to support the organization's goals
Think and Act Globally—identify and weigh factors that might contribute to or interfere with success and the implications of actions on others	Misses some of the risk factors Fails to elicit others' input on how to identify and manage risk	Identifies the factors that might be at risk or present risk and works with manager and other stakeholders on how to control it	Develops alternative scenarios to forecast impact and problems

TOOL 4.3D: JOB AID FOR DESCRIBING BEHAVIORS BY JOB LEVEL AND LEVEL OF PERFORMANCE—SUPERVISOR

| Competencies | Supervisor | | | Your Rating: | | | Your Rationale |
	Needs Development 1	Effective 2	Highly Effective 3	1	2	3	
Problem Solve—obtain sufficient data to analyze a situation and draw conclusions from which to develop a plan of action or provide an answer	Misses the point Fails to seek information Focuses on one solution Concentrates on the easily understood Delays or makes snap judgments	Gets to what is relevant Obtains enough information to understand the issues Considers one or more alternatives Timing of decisions is appropriate	Grasps the complexities Goes after the critical information Considers two or more alternatives Makes decisions in face of time constraints or uncertainty				
Create—spot things that need to be changed, recognize where improvement will help, and conceive of new ideas or programs to meet organizational needs	Modifies components or processes based on a cursory review of the existing ones Specifications are too general to implement or only meet some of the requirements Designs or modifications address simple problems Designs have little or no use beyond the immediate problem	Reviews existing components or processes prior to modifying them Specifications meet the requirements Designs or modifications meet needs of more complex problems Designs are flexible and have some alternative use	Thoroughly reviews the relevant existing components or systems prior to modifying them Provides detailed specifications that satisfy the identified requirements Designs work for complex problems Designs are flexible and have alternative uses				

(Continued)

Competency			
Plan—identify and describe the activities, resources, and timeline necessary to accomplish a goal	Fails to set completion dates Fails to identify key activities Does not establish budget Focuses on one aspect of the plan without identifying other key activities	Outlines projects with completion dates Identifies key activities Identifies budget requirements	Reviews and identifies critical milestones Links milestones to budget and aligns plans with other initiatives Acts on opportunities to reduce budget Timeline and budget meet requirements
Implement—carry out the activities required to accomplish a goal	Desired results or objectives are vague, roles are not well-defined Defines scope in ways that over- or underestimates what is required Acts without a plan Provides too few resources or provides them only after significant delays Incurs delays due to lack of direction, clarity, or other reasons Spends time on low priority projects or activities Delegates inappropriately	Identifies the results and objectives and defines the scope Plans have action steps, sequences, and timetables Provides resources Delegates work per plan Sets priorities based on plan Arranges own work so as to execute plans efficiently	Accurately defines project scope Sets clear, measurable objectives Anticipates potential resistance to change and plans strategies to overcome it Translates objectives into executable plans Confirms resources are available in advance to avoid delays Delegates appropriately and provides sufficient instruction

TOOL 4.3D: JOB AID FOR DESCRIBING BEHAVIORS BY JOB LEVEL AND LEVEL OF PERFORMANCE—SUPERVISOR (Continued)

Competencies	Supervisor			Your Rating:			Your Rationale
	Needs Development 1	Effective 2	Highly Effective 3	1	2	3	
Advise—give advice to help resolve individual and organization issues	When facilitating meetings mixes making evaluative statements about the content with facilitating the process Fails to adequately represent special interests' needs when mediating Fails to lead people to consider other alternatives	When facilitating meetings, separates the role of participant from that of facilitator States ideas and feelings of special interests Helps people to be open to alternatives	When facilitating meetings, balances the content (task) with process (what is happening) Accurately represents special interests and gains acceptance Asks open-ended questions Clearly states the alternatives				
Communicate—inform others of observations, requirements, and expectations using multiple media and channels	Shares information with inappropriate people, fails to share with those who are, or shares too late Has to be sought out for information Displays poor active listening skills Messages are confusing, not well-organized Appears awkward, has distracting mannerisms	Shares specific relevant information with those who need to know at the appropriate time Uses effective listening techniques Shares information across boundaries on major issues Hears others out Actively listens Puts points across, thoughts are well-organized Uses multiple channels	Consistently communicates across boundaries Effectively uses multiple channels and media to assure messages are received and considered				

Build and Use Relationships—establish trust and mutual respect that result in productive relationships	Appears aloof Focuses on the task without building rapport Shows no interest in dealing with others outside of own level, background, site Does not reaffirm relationships Does not follow through on commitments Does not respond to others' concerns, opinions Expresses disagreement bluntly, avoids conflict	Cooperative Initiates building rapport Builds and works to sustain relationships with people in the industry Follows through on commitments and advises others on the need for extensions and so forth Is open to others' concerns, opinions Acknowledges conflicts	Projects sincerity, openness Initiates interaction and conversation Builds and preserves relationships with people across levels, backgrounds, site, industry Follows through on commitments Seeks to understand others' concerns, opinions Expresses disagreement tactfully and addresses it straightforwardly
Lead—provide consistent direction and support so others stay focused on what is important	Caves in Does not assert ideas or positions on issues Does not convey conviction Gets few results or results have negative impact Is unproductive, accomplishes little Expectations are vague, roles unclear or in conflict	Exemplifies the behaviors wanted in others Communicates objectives and links work to the objectives Generally persists Asserts own ideas on critical issues Conveys conviction on most ideas Obtains results that meet current expectations	Consistently exemplifies the behaviors wanted in others Persists Tactfully asserts own position Conveys personal conviction Obtains results that have a positive impact on the business Maintains consistent productivity

(Continued)

TOOL 4.3D: JOB AID FOR DESCRIBING BEHAVIORS BY JOB LEVEL AND LEVEL OF PERFORMANCE—SUPERVISOR (Continued)

Competencies	Supervisor			Your Rating:			Your Rationale
	Needs Development 1	Effective 2	Highly Effective 3	1	2	3	
	Does not give feedback Fails to gain others' support Makes little or no attempt to build enthusiasm or to gain understanding	Meets important commitments Gives clear directions Prone to give positive rather than negative feedback Gains others' support Tries to build enthusiasm and gain understanding	Sets clear expectations Gives specific and useful feedback Gains others' enthusiastic support through compelling arguments Fosters enthusiasm and understanding				
Cooperate—collaborate with others in ways that accomplish goals and lead to meaningful results	Participation is minimal, conveys disinterest Develops own ideas and rarely changes based on discussions with others Does not encourage people to work together Conveys a lack of confidence in others Tightly controls personal resources Provides some support to cross-functional initiatives Acts in ways that benefit self but may be detrimental to other groups	Participates when asked Modifies own thinking based on input from others Encourages people to work together Conveys confidence in others Offers personal resources Participates in cross-functional meetings Seeks the approval of some stakeholders	Looks for opportunities to participate Incorporates the ideas of others into own Encourages others to draw on people with different ideas Conveys confidence in others Shares resources Facilitates cross-functional meetings Works to reach consensus				

Competency			
Develop Self and Others—learns and helps others learn	Does not engage in developmental activities Tries to avoid receiving any feedback; deflects or rationalizes when given feedback; does not adapt behavior in response to feedback Does only what is expected	Has a developmental plan Accepts all feedback, adapts behavior in response to feedback Takes on new work challenges as available or assigned	Follows through on developmental plan Solicits good and bad feedback, takes action to prevent future mistakes Seeks out new work challenges
Think and Act Strategically—identify pressures and their implications on a specific course of action and ways to circumvent them	Fails to reference external factors Lacks awareness of broader strategic issues and business needs Focuses efforts on activities that have little bearing on the organization's strategic direction	Discusses and considers the significance of external factors Proposes plans and decisions that consider the business' needs Keeps day-to-day issues aligned with strategic objectives	Can accurately represent the significance of external factors Recommends actions that contribute to supporting business needs Ensures actions are aligned with the business' strategic objectives

(Continued)

TOOL 4.3D: JOB AID FOR DESCRIBING BEHAVIORS BY JOB LEVEL AND LEVEL OF PERFORMANCE—SUPERVISOR (Continued)

Competencies	Needs Development 1	Supervisor Effective 2	Highly Effective 3	Your Rating: 1	2	3	Your Rationale
Think and Act Globally—identify and weigh factors that might contribute to or interfere with success and the implications of actions on others	Rarely sees the risk Takes actions or makes decisions that cause unnecessary risk Inaccurately quantifies the risks and consequences; bases assessment on erroneous assumptions Forecasts are inaccurate, incomplete, or vague; offers few if any alternatives Delays or hesitates under time constraints and times of uncertainty	Recognizes and considers risk before taking action Quantifies technical risks and consequences Forecasts risks and rewards and provides viable options Decides on a course of action when faced with time constraints or uncertainty Makes decisions of some consequence based on an analysis of the risk involved	Openly considers the risks before acting Accurately quantifies risk and consequences in concrete terms so management can make informed decisions Develops risk assessment models so management has viable options Acts decisively in the face of time constraints and uncertainty Makes decisions of significant risk based on the available data				

TOOL 4.3E: JOB AID FOR DESCRIBING BEHAVIORS BY JOB LEVEL AND LEVEL OF PERFORMANCE—INDIVIDUAL CONTRIBUTOR

Competencies	Individual Contributor			Your Rating:			Your Rationale
	Needs Development 1	Effective 2	Highly Effective 3	1	2	3	
Problem Solve—obtain sufficient data to analyze a situation and draw conclusions from which to develop a plan of action or provide an answer	Misses the point Fails to seek information Fails to confirm the accuracy of information States opinion without the facts	Probes for what is relevant Obtains enough information to understand the point Summarizes and interprets the data Suggests solutions or actions based on the data	Begins to grasp the complexities Knows when the critical information is missing Points out discrepancies in data				
Create—spot things that need to be changed, recognize where improvement will help, and conceive of new ideas or programs to meet organizational needs	Recommends modifications to components or processes based on a cursory review of the existing ones Poses specifications that are too general to implement or only meet some of the requirements	Reviews existing components or processes prior to recommending modifications Suggests useful specifications Considers the need for flexibility and alternative uses when offering design suggestions	Thoroughly reviews the relevant existing components or systems prior to recommending any modifications Adds detail to specifications to confirm they will satisfy the identified requirements Identifies how to make designs more flexible or have alternative uses				

(Continued)

TOOL 4.3E: JOB AID FOR DESCRIBING BEHAVIORS BY JOB LEVEL AND LEVEL OF PERFORMANCE—INDIVIDUAL CONTRIBUTOR (Continued)

Competencies	Individual Contributor			Your Rating:			Your Rationale
	Needs Development 1	Effective 2	Highly Effective 3	1	2	3	
Plan—identify and describe the activities, resources, and timeline necessary to accomplish a goal	Fails to confirm expectation around completion dates. Fails to confirm what the key activities are. Does not recognize how added activities or missed deadlines affect budget	Outlines smaller-scale projects with completion dates. Adds the key activities. Confirms budget requirements. Does recognize when the budget will be affected	Outlines very large-scale or complex projects. Points out barriers to meeting plans. Seeks help before budget is negatively impacted. Suggests opportunities to reduce budget				
Implement—carry out the activities required to accomplish a goal	Fails to clarify vague objectives or ill-defined roles. Accepts the scope and the resource estimate without question. Incurs delays due to lack of resources or direction. Spends time on low-priority activities	Confirms the results, objectives, and scope. Confirms understanding of action steps, sequences, and timetable. Requests resources when needed. Sets priorities based on plan	Recognizes discrepancies in objectives, scope, time lines, and resource availability. Makes objectives clearer and more measurable. Builds personal work plans so can meet commitments				
Advise—give advice to help resolve individual and organization issues	Fails to maintain contact with all levels. Fails to keep management informed. Personally assumes or shifts responsibility inappropriately	Maintains contact with all levels. Represents the ideas and feelings of special interests. Helps people to commit to act	Helps others accept difficult information. Asks probing questions. Helps others accept responsibility for own actions				

Communicate—inform others of observations, requirements, and expectations using multiple media and channels	Shares inappropriate information Has to be sought out for information Displays poor active listening skills Messages are insensitive Appears awkward, has distracting mannerisms Uses few or a limited number of media	Shares specific relevant information with those who need to know at the appropriate time Does not interrupt, lets others finish their points Actively listens Puts points across, thoughts are well-organized Uses the appropriate media	Is facile in communicating to different audiences who have different needs, interests, and motives Leverages media to support goal
Build and Use Relationships—establish trust and mutual respect that results in productive relationships	Fails to take time to build rapport Shows no interest in building relationships with people outside of own function Does not follow through on commitments Does not respond to others' concerns, opinions Avoids conflict	Builds and works to sustain relationships with people at all levels in the unit Follows through on commitments or seeks help before relationships are jeopardized Is open to others' concerns, opinions Acknowledges conflicts	Projects sincerity, openness Seeks to understand others' concerns, opinions Expresses disagreement tactfully and addresses it straightforwardly

(Continued)

TOOL 4.3E: JOB AID FOR DESCRIBING BEHAVIORS BY JOB LEVEL AND LEVEL OF PERFORMANCE—INDIVIDUAL CONTRIBUTOR (Continued)

Competencies	Individual Contributor			Your Rating:			Your Rationale
	Needs Development 1	Effective 2	Highly Effective 3	1	2	3	
Lead—provide consistent direction and support so others stay focused on what is important	Does not take a position on issues, or takes a position based on insufficient data; Does not convey conviction; Fails to meet important commitments; Fails to gain others' support and makes no attempt to build enthusiasm or to gain understanding	Does take a position on issues when is informed; Conveys conviction on most ideas; Meets important commitments; Gains others' support by gaining their understanding; Leads by example	Identifies key issues and seeks ways to take an informed position; Conveys personal conviction; Exemplifies leadership behaviors; Fosters enthusiasm and understanding that results in support				
Cooperate—collaborate with others in ways that accomplish goals and lead to meaningful results	When asked to join a team, participation is minimal; Rarely discusses ideas with others; Conveys a lack of confidence or disinterest in others; Acts in ways that benefit self but may be detrimental to the group	Actively participates on teams; Seeks others' ideas to help shape own; Conveys confidence in others; Helps keep the group on task while preserving inner team relationships	Looks for opportunities to participate or facilitate; Polls others' opinions without sacrificing own perspective; Conveys confidence in others; Helps facilitate meetings; Works to reach consensus				
Develop Self and Others—learn and help others learn	Seeks developmental activities with little relevance to current job or developmental need; Does what is expected	Participates in developmental activities; Accepts feedback; Takes on new work challenges as available or assigned	Builds own developmental plan; Seeks opportunities to compare own performance or knowledge with others in order to learn				

				Seeks out new work challenges
Think and Act Strategically—identify pressures and their implications on a specific course of action and ways to circumvent them	Fails to consider limitations Lacks awareness of broader business unit issues or needs Focuses people's attention on activities of low priority or that have little bearing on the unit's goals	Discusses and considers the significance of internal challenges, strengths, and limitations Adds comments to plans and decisions based on the needs of the unit Keeps day-to-day issues aligned with unit's goals	Understands the significance of current and future challenges, yet looks beyond them Recommends actions that support the unit's needs Ensures own actions are aligned with the business unit's goals	
Think and Act Globally—identify and weigh factors that might contribute to or interfere with success and the implications of actions on others	Rarely sees the connection between failure to execute a plan or procedure and the risk Behaves in ways that cause unnecessary risk Fails to see the connection between own behavior and its effect on relationships Stalls or delays when time constraints are tight	Sees the connection between action or inaction and risk to relationships, budget, and so on Own behaviors do not put relationships at risk Recognizes the potential risk associated with new procedures or policies Acts appropriately when faced with time constraints	Seeks to quantify the risks associated with actions or inaction Studies risk-assessment models developed to help management compare viable options	

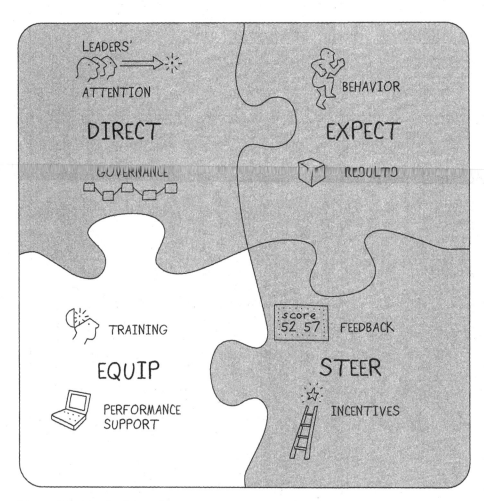

Figure 5.1. Leadership Roles

Lynn Kearny, CPT, Graphic Recorder

Chapter 5

How to Use Orientations and Training Effectively

How do I learn to do this?
Who can I ask if I have a question?

One of the biggest challenges managers and supervisors face is how to bring people up-to-speed as quickly as possible. Some organizations spend years training people to do the job. Other organizations try to hire people with some degree of readiness; however, all organizations find they must share in the responsibility for helping people become proficient as quickly as possible. People are proficient when they can do a job or task consistently to an acceptable level under normal circumstances. The role of managers and supervisors in equipping people for the job is in areas of orientation, readiness assessment, formal training, and on-the-job training.

This chapter is about how to make the best use of these methods for preparing people.

PERFORMANCE IMPROVEMENT

From a performance improvement perspective, people deserve opportunities to learn the job. Training should be relevant and timely, and there should be ways for people to obtain the information they need when they need it and in a form they can easily use. However, this requires someone to be responsible for studying the job and people in the job to identify (1) what people have to know and (2) what people may already know and do well, so that money and time are not wasted on unnecessary training.

COMMON MISSTEPS

Here are some of the mistakes managers and supervisors make that limit the effectiveness of investments intended to make people productive:

1. They fail to put a particular person in charge of new employee orientation to assure the new people's attention is on what is important and to make

that person accountable for how well people are integrated into the work unit.

2. They are not clear about what problems they want training to solve and do not confirm that training is the appropriate solution.

3. They do not meet with their people prior to taking training to explain what is expected of them when they return to the job.

4. They do not meet with their people after training to review what was covered and what type of on-the-job support is required to reinforce what was learned.

5. They fail to observe their people after training to determine whether the training was effective.

ORIENTATION

Orientation is about starting off a new assignment in the best way. It is the process of aligning people's expectations and attention with what is important in terms of working with others and being clear about how and what work should be done. Some expectations were set during the hiring process; therefore, it is important to know what those were. For example, promises may have been inferred about how much travel the job involves, the types of tools and equipment the person would have access to, and so forth. Orientation should be planned, not ad hoc, as it is during the initial hours and days on the job that perceptions are formed and decisions made about what is expected, who is in charge, and how valued someone is. First impressions are hard to change.

Orientation should be thought of as a process, not an event. For example, reference materials, such as lists of who to contact, should be designed for use long after the "formal" orientation. Orientation can be thought of as in three phases. The first phase is about answering the new hire's personal questions, such as how to get paid, enroll in health insurance, where to work, what equipment he or she will use, where to eat lunch, and so forth.

The second phase is about assessing people's readiness to do the job. This includes finding out how much they know and can do and how much training or coaching is required to bring them to proficiency. The third phase is becoming acclimated to the job, co-workers, and the work tools. Even experienced hires require some orientation, as they do not always bring sufficient knowledge about the organization's processes, products, and procedures to become productive quickly. Less experienced hires require even more guidance before they can be productive. Here is what should happen during orientation. People should:

1. Learn where things are located, how to find their way around, and some of the basic work protocols.

2. Become acquainted with the organization's information and communication systems.

3. Be introduced to the tools they will use on the job.

4. Learn all of the safety rules and regulations, be shown how to use equipment safely, and be enrolled in any appropriate safety training program.

5. Meet co-workers, customers, and bosses and gain a deeper understanding about what is expected of them by each one.

6. Learn about their support system, including the union steward, procedural manuals, benefits administrator, and the employee assistance program administrator.

7. Be introduced to the structure of the organization, its customers, industry standing, products and services, vision, mission, and brand identity so they know for whom they work.

8. Be allowed to express doubt about their decision to accept the job or assignment.

9. Have some type of skills and knowledge review to determine whether training or coaching is necessary.

The result is that people form judgments about everyone's status, who and what are really valued, and where they fit in. It is in forming these judgments that people seek to reconfirm the wisdom of their decision to accept the assignment and reconcile any discrepancies or doubts. A mistake some organizations make is that they use the orientation to "sell" the job and set up unrealistic expectations that later result in disappointment.

From the organization's perspective, orientation serves two purposes as well. It is the time to find out whether the person can work effectively with the group and to facilitate the person becoming productive as quickly as possible. Therefore, someone should be responsible and accountable for orienting new people to the work unit. The orientation should cover more than human resource's paperwork and housekeeping. It is also a time to give people some history of the company, the role of the work unit, a perspective on the unit's customers, and a briefing on the kinds of tools that are used in accomplishing the work.

READINESS CHECK

The purpose of a readiness check is to find out whether training is needed and how much training or coaching people require for them to work independently at the job. It can be as formal as a series of skills and knowledge tests or as simple as a self-assessment where people check themselves or observe others. If people are being asked to do a task that there is no other possible way for them to learn but on the job, then an assessment is unnecessary, as you know they require training. However, if they might have learned parts or all of the required skills in a previous job situation or through training, you might want to confirm how much they remember and what is applicable to your specific application. You then would use the results to learn:

- Whether the organization's formal new hire training or an education program is appropriate
- Whether the person can be exempted from some or all of the formal new hire training program
- An appropriate source for the training, including your organization, professional or trade associations, a private vendor, or an academic institution
- Whether on-the-job training is sufficient
- Whether self-directed training is sufficient, where people are given manuals, CD-ROM disks, and like material to learn on their own

Here are some guidelines for leveraging the time during orientation to help bring people to proficiency faster.

TOOL 5.1: HOW TO ORIENT NEW EMPLOYEES

Purpose

These guidelines are designed to help you make the most out of the time spent orienting people to the organization, team, and job.

How

With members of your team and perhaps someone from human resources or training, and safety, if appropriate:

A. List all of the things you want to accomplish through the orientation. Be sure to consider:

   1. How and when you will assess the new person's readiness to assume the new role
   2. The tools and systems the person will use
   3. Any rules there may be about how work is done, including safety and documentation requirements
   4. The history of the organization, including its product breakthroughs, heroes, and legends
   5. The organization's product and service mix

6. The organization's customers, competitors, and partners

7. The industry standing of the organization

8. Introductions to the people he or she will be working with

9. The behaviors and accomplishments that indicate the person fits in with the group and is learning the job

B. If you decide to assess a person's readiness, work with someone in training or HR and consider:

1. What specific skills and knowledge you want the readiness check to determine

2. What standard assessment tools may be available for purchase from a trade or professional association or a private vendor

3. Who will conduct the readiness check and at what point during the orientation it will be done

4. How the results will be used, for example, to create a personal development plan or to exempt the person from specific courses or units currently in the new hire training program

C. When a person joins your team, assign a couple of people to be responsible for different aspects of the initial thirty, sixty, and ninety days on the job. The people should be good role models and care about helping the new person become successful. The goal is for the new person to establish more than one relationship so that, if one of those relationships should become strained or end for whatever reason, the new person has a bridge to the rest of the group and does not feel like an outsider. Assigning more than one person to help with the orientation can also speed up the integration of the new employee into the group.

1. Make one person responsible for the orientation overall; this person can play another role as well

2. One person can handle the logistics, from filling out the paperwork, finding identification tags and parking stickers, and learning where to store personal belongings and where to eat lunch

3. Someone else can handle introductions and explain what everyone does

4. Perhaps another person can explain the tools and systems used and what the job is about while observing someone doing one aspect of the job

5. If you want the new hire to go through some type of readiness test, someone should be responsible for setting it up, coordinating the effort, and explaining how the results will be used

6. Everyone should make himself or herself available to answer questions and take turns accompanying the person to lunch and breaks

D. Greet the new person yourself and spend time with him or her the first day on the job or shortly thereafter to show that you are accessible.

1. Set some milestones for the first thirty, sixty, and ninety days, those behaviors or accomplishments you want to see as evidence the person will fit in and be able to contribute effectively (therefore take time to identify what you want to see happen)

2. You might ask the person after the first month what his or her goals are for the job (If the person is very young or inexperienced in the workplace, you may have to suggest some goals. The less experienced the person about the world of work, the more important it is to properly lay the groundwork)

3. Make it a point to observe the person doing some aspect of the job, whether it is executing a procedure or communicating with co-workers or customers

E. Periodically check in with the person, specifically meeting at the thirty-, sixty-, and ninety-day points to discuss concerns and progress. There should be no surprises.

Hint: Set up one or more lunches where co-workers take turns sharing stories or tidbits of information about the job, the company, and customers that they found helpful. Recognize the people who were assigned to be responsible for some aspect of the orientation.

TRAINING

Training can make a difference if there is a lack of skills and knowledge. However, training is not a substitute for clear directions, realistic expectations of what the work environment can provide, appropriate performance measures, good feedback, or adequate workspace or materials. When training is appropriate, it is important to recognize that not all training is equal, because it is done for different reasons. Some training just conveys information; other training builds skills; and still other training is meant to be motivational or inspirational. New hire training, for example, usually includes information about company policies and, depending on the level of the job, it may include extensive training on the job's procedures or equipment. Training that is done to comply with federal or local regulations, such as Hazmat, may build skills, but it more likely explains rules about what to do and not do under certain circumstances. Still other training is done for professional or career development reasons. Rarely should training be done to correct poor performance unless the cause is known to be a lack of knowledge or skill.

Characteristics of Effective Training

Effective training has the following characteristics:

- Clear explanations of the main points, especially the rules about what people should and should not do. Explanations of why the topic is relevant and important to people.

- Examples of doing something correctly and incorrectly (If you only have one type of example, people do not learn how to make distinctions or learn how to discriminate between something that is done well or done poorly).

- Examples of appropriately following a rule or a procedure and inappropriately doing it; examples with explanations help people understand what to do, why, and under what circumstances.

- Opportunities to practice applying the rules or doing a procedure under conditions that are most similar to the job (except in the case where people's safety might be jeopardized). *It is practice that builds skills.* If the practice is missing or minimal, it means people will practice back on the job, which will require you to provide greater supervision or assign the person a partner who is already proficient and can provide coaching.

- Ways for people to receive feedback about how well they did, through tests, role plays, or peer evaluations. The important thing is for people to find out whether they are progressing appropriately.

- Quick reference guides or job aids that can be used back on the job to help people recall how to do a procedure or when to apply a rule (see the next chapter for more on this subject).

Job training is usually done in one of two ways, formally or informally. *Formal* job training includes workshops, seminars, conferences, and academic courses that may be offered by training or human resource departments, training vendors, or academic institutions. Formal training is frequently done in a classroom setting, yet an increasing amount of is being delivered electronically (computer, web, audiotape, and videotape). Some training makes use of a combination of self-study (read manuals or information online) followed by a structured group study where the learner meets with a trainer or facilitator in a physical or virtual classroom. *Informal* training is usually done on the job under the guidance of the supervisor or a co-worker who is already proficient.

Formal Training

Whether you want your people to attend a program developed by your organization or from another source, such as a professional association, you should ask to see the learning objectives and the plan for accomplishing them. Learning objectives describe what the learner should know or do differently as a result of having completed the program and how that learning will be tested or confirmed. The learning plan describes how the content and skills will be explained, demonstrated, and practiced.

Prior to any training (whether it be offered by the organization or another source), meet with your people and discuss your expectations, including:

- Why they are going to training
- What you expect them to learn
- How the new knowledge or skill might show up on the job
- How the content relates to the goals of the organization
- What you need to provide after the training to reinforce the application of the new skills and knowledge
- Whether or not you want them to share what was learned with others

Once the training is complete, follow up on your commitments and on theirs. Here are some guidelines for getting the most out of formal workshops, conferences, and academic sponsored programs.

TOOL 5.2: HOW TO GET THE MOST FROM TRAINING

Purpose

Organizations spend a lot of money on training, yet people's behavior does not always change as expected. This set of guidelines will help assure you receive your money's worth.

How

Work with the person responsible from training or human resources to better understand the purpose of the program, the problem it is expected to resolve, or what deficiency it is intended to eliminate to determine how likely it is to accomplish the learning objectives.

A. Evaluate the training yourself or be assured that someone else has done so.
  1. Confirm what the objectives are (a) to inform; (b) to motivate or inspire; and (c) to build skills.
  2. Ask to see the objectives. The objectives should specify what people will know or do as a result of completing the program and what the measures are of learning. You want to know what the student will do, not what the instructor will do.

3. Ask what percent of the time is spent on explanations, demonstrations (this includes stories), and practice with feedback. The more the program professes to build skills, the more time should be spent on practice with feedback. Ask:

   a. How is the information relevant to the learner and the organization? (inform)

   b. How is the information to be used on the job? (inform)

   c. Are new behaviors expected and, if so, how will they be reinforced back on the job? (motivate or inspire)

   d. What are the consequences if people's behavior does not change? (motivate or inspire)

   e. What is the incentive for people to change? (motivate or inspire)

   f. How many opportunities are there to practice? (skills)

   g. Are there pre-tests so people know what to focus on during the training? (skills)

   h. Are there tests at key points or at the end of the training so people know how well they are doing? (skills)

   i. Are there training materials that can be used on the job as quick reference guides to help people recall the rules and procedures? (skills)

4. If the training is for new hires, purposefully pay attention to:

   a. How long after the formal training it takes for a person to become fully proficient on the job, as this gives you a truer measure of the effectiveness of the training.

   b. The amount of extra support the person requires, whether from you or from a co-worker, and for how long, as this gives you a truer measure of the cost of the training.

   c. The types of questions people ask after training, as this may be an indication that the training is not clear about certain rules or procedures or the need for on-the-job support materials.

   d. The number of times you have to correct what a person does, as this may be an indication the training is not explaining the way a job should be done as you would like it to be done.

5. Tell human resources or training what additional support was required to help the person do the job and, if the level of support was excessive, work with them to improve the quality of the program.

B. Prepare the person before the training. Before people leave work to attend training or go to a conference:

1. Ask them to identify what they want to get from the program, whether it is information, confirmation, inspiration, or new skills

2. Tell them if you have something specific you want them to learn and what you want to see them doing differently as a result

3. Ask them to be prepared to brief you and their co-workers on their return on what they learned and how the organization might benefit from the new information, procedure, or whatever, encouraging them to pay attention and making them responsible for their own learning

C. Meet after the training.

1. Ask the person to brief you on what happened and what he or she learned

2. Talk about what was learned and how it will benefit the person, the team, the department, or the organization

3. Ask how confident the person feels he or she is in the ability to perform the skills taught in the training

4. Find out what you can do to support or reinforce what was learned and honor your commitment

D. Meet with the training department and discuss the possibility of their briefing you on how well your people did during the sessions, especially for programs offered by the organization

Hint: If the purpose of the training is to update your people on changes in the organization's products, processes, or customer promises, be sure to help your people understand what they should do differently after the training. Set time aside to talk with them about how their jobs are affected and what type of support might be required for them to be successful.

PROFESSIONAL STAFF AND ANNUAL CONFERENCES

Karen supervises a professional staff of nine. Four are senior and five are new, both to the company and to the field. Every year when the budget is being prepared, staff asks that money be set aside to attend professional conferences. Karen's goal is for everyone to attend at least one professional conference per year, but not necessarily the same conference. She meets with her people to review the year's goals and to discuss which conferences would be more likely to have sessions that would support the work being done. Staff identifies what they want to learn, find out more about, or accomplish by going to a conference. Two goals that repeatedly come up are (1) to find out what is new in the discipline and (2) to compare vendors. She asks that they monitor the conference programs and present a business case on why they should go to the one they selected, how they and the company will benefit, and in what ways this particular conference is better than others. Once she agrees, she stipulates that they must brief her and the rest of the staff on what was learned and the implications on the work being done when they return.

TECHNICAL STAFF AND CERTIFICATION

David manages a group of ten field technicians. The technicians service, repair, and troubleshoot customers' mechanical systems. David's training plan for his crews includes mandated safety training, briefings on technical updates, and continuing education credits required to maintain their certifications.

David works with his training department to discuss how to obtain the training his crews require at the least cost and disruption of work. The training department negotiates with the local community college to conduct safety classes. David requires his crew who attend to prepare a fifteen-minute update on what was covered and that they present it at the next monthly staff meeting. David also requires each of his crew once a year to deliver a thirty-minute troubleshooting update at one of the monthly staff meetings. He also asks that someone from engineering or product development deliver an update in conjunction with the release of a new product or a product enhancement. To support his technicians' continuing education requirements, David monitors the self-study programs offered by the trade associations and either leases or purchases programs that he thinks might be of value. The technicians can check out the programs; however, they must study them on their own time. His rationale is that the employee carries the certification with him or her and should somehow share in the cost of maintaining it.

On-the-Job Training

Most people learn their jobs by observing others. People learn to emulate what others do. Therefore it is especially important that they copy the right behaviors. When people learn by observing others you risk their picking up some undesirable shortcuts. The best on-the-job training is planned. Here is a suggested phased approach to doing on-the-job training.

Phase I—Establish the Context. Tell people what the job is about. If the job is part of a larger process, you might, for example, walk the person through the process as if he or she were a product being made, a problem being solved, or the paperwork being completed. It is important for him or her to gain an overview of what the group does as a whole, where the job fits into the process, and why the job or task exists.

Phase II—Observe. Allow the learner to observe one or more people who do the task or job well, doing all or just some aspect of the job. Ask the person being observed to talk out loud (or you do it), explaining each step, why it is done, and why it is important. If possible give the learner a performance checklist with all of the attributes of a job done well. Allow the learner to observe the task again or to observe another person. Talk about what is the same or different.

Phase III—Guided Practice. Next, allow the "learner" to do one or more parts of the task or job. However, have someone by his or her side explaining exactly what to do. If possible, let the new hire use written procedures, quick reference guides, or other tools to help remember specific steps or a sequence of steps. Whenever an error is made, have the learner go back and redo the step until it is done correctly. Repeat this until the learner gains sufficient proficiency to do the job with little or no coaching. If you work in a union environment, you may have to modify this phase to comply with your agreement; however, do work with the union steward to arrange for ways for people to get "hands-on" practice with strong guidance.

Phase IV—Practice. Now let the person continue to do the job or task while being observed. The co-worker who is doing the training now gives feedback on the quality of the product and the appropriateness of the behavior and is available for questions. Remember, it is practice with feedback that builds proficiency.

Phase V—Follow-Up Observation. Conduct periodic observations to confirm that the person is following the guidelines and progressing in the job.

Repeat all of the phases until the person has learned all aspects of the job and can work independently. Here are some guidelines for doing on-the-job training.

TOOL 5.3: HOW TO MAKE ON-THE-JOB TRAINING MORE EFFECTIVE

Purpose
This guideline is designed to help you be more purposeful when doing or managing on-the-job training.

How
With your staff and perhaps someone from training:

A. Identify one or more persons to be responsible for coordinating the on-the-job training. This person could be different from the one who actually conducts the on-the-job training. It should be part of his or her performance review criteria.

B. Decide how to best establish the context of the job or task and show where it fits into the bigger picture.

C. Chunk the job or task into smaller teachable parts.

D. Create some visuals, checklists, or job aids to help people remember the steps, recognize good work from work that is not good, and eventually check their own work (see the next chapter for more on this topic).

E. Come up with a timeline noting how far you want people to be on the learning curve by certain dates in the future.

F. Identify someone with the patience to explain each behavior, activity, or step and the willingness and ability to give people meaningful feedback. Remember, the best performer is not necessarily the best teacher. Training others should be part of his or her performance review.

G. Develop a set of rules to help the person doing the training and the learner, such as:

1. If you make a mistake you have to go back and redo or repeat the step

2. If you do not understand, keep asking until you do

3. If you can think of a better way to document the steps or show how something is done, speak up and we will help you develop it

H. Develop a performance checklist of either the behaviors or product attributes that will be used to judge the adequacy of the work and let the person see it.

I. Find out whether the "teacher" would like other tools or quick reference guides to help explain key steps, procedures, and so forth (see the next chapter for more about this topic).

J. Periodically, meet with the person doing the on-the-job training to find out how the "teacher" is holding up and what he or she might need from you.

K. Periodically, meet with the learner to listen to his or her concerns.

L. Be sure to recognize and commend the person doing the training and let others know of his or her success (see the chapter on how to recognize and reward performance).

Hint: Keep track of how long it takes people to function independently without error. This will give you a better estimate in the future of the number and types of resources you require to develop new people. Recognize the people who contributed time and information to helping others become proficient faster.

TIPS

Here are some suggestions on how to better equip your people so they are more productive and become proficient faster.

1. Take the time to learn about the training offered and promoted by your organization. Be a better consumer. Ask for proof that the programs have the features required to deliver the promised results.

2. Challenge why training takes so long, but understand that, if you want your people to be more skilled, it takes time. They can either learn in training or on the job, but the learning has to take place at some time.

SUMMARY

People deserve the information they require to perform. They also deserve the opportunity to be trained on how to do the job in the best way possible. Giving people what they require means managers and supervisors have to step up to the responsibility of challenging what people should learn and how to best learn it. They should be more astute consumers of training and better deliverers of on-the-job training. Managers and supervisors cannot afford to defer to tradition and rely on training or human resources to do it without their involvement. Training and human resources bring special expertise, but the manager and supervisor make the training work.

WHERE TO LEARN MORE

Here are some quick, easy reads with useful information you can apply.

Mager, R.F. *Goal Analysis* (Atlanta, GA: Center for Effective Performance, 1997). About 130 pages, paperback.

Mager, R.F. *What Every Manager Should Know About Training* (Atlanta, GA: Center for Effective Performance, 1999). About 140 pages, paperback.

Mager, R.F., and Pipe, P. *Analyzing Performance Problems* (Atlanta, GA: Center for Effective Performance, 1997). About 140 pages, paperback.

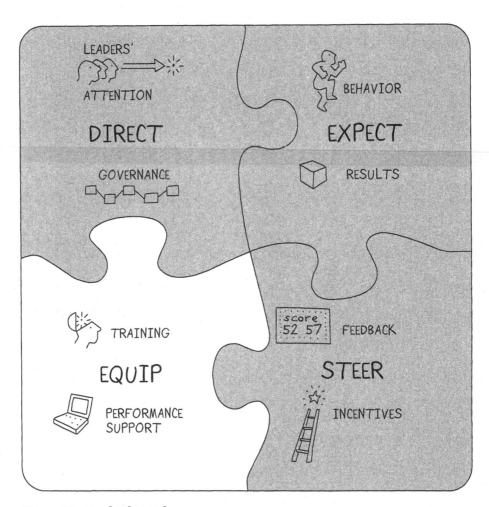

Figure 6.1. Leadership Roles

Lynn Kearny, CPT, Graphic Recorder

Chapter 6

How to Use Job Aids to Support Performance

Are there any easier ways to do this? So what are the rules?

*O*rganizations spend millions of dollars on facilities, equipment, and information and on communication systems so their people can do the work necessary to stay in business. Yet they overlook the importance of evaluating the functionality of standards and work rules and the contributions of performance support tools to help people learn their jobs more quickly and perform to standard more consistently. Managers' and supervisors' role is to give the appropriate people feedback on the functionality of the workspace, equipment, and systems. They must also help evaluate the usefulness of and advocate for the availability and improvement of *job aids or quick reference guides, job templates, standards,* and *work rules and procedures.*

This chapter is about how to make the best use of these methods for helping people gain proficiency more quickly and perform more consistently.

PERFORMANCE IMPROVEMENT

From a performance improvement perspective, facilities, equipment, tools, and the like are essential; however, some things should be done for each of them to live up to expectations. Workspace and layout, for example, should be designed to support the requirements of the job, not be entitlements for seniority or position status. This means someone should be responsible for studying how work is done to identify the behaviors the space is expected to support. Equipment should have the functionality required to support the tasks people perform. This means someone should be responsible for confirming what is required to do the tasks and that the equipment has the expected functions.

From a performance improvement perspective, work rules, job aids, templates, and standards should help people be more efficient. However, this requires someone to be responsible for taking the time to study the job and people in the job to identify and evaluate the effectiveness of the work rules, job aids, templates, and standards.

COMMON MISSTEPS Here are some of the mistakes managers and supervisors make that limit the effectiveness of investments intended to make people productive:

1. They fail to ask questions of and work with the appropriate person in facilities, quality, or industrial engineering to do a study of the workflow and activities to identify people's surface space, floor space, and layout requirements.

2. They do not work with the appropriate person in quality or industrial engineering to diagram the work processes and identify ways to streamline them to reduce errors, reduce cycle time, and improve the quality of the outputs.

3. They fail to work with the appropriate person in labor relations to identify and evaluate work rules.

4. They do not work with the appropriate person in human resources or training to create job aids and other support materials to reinforce the skills learned during training.

5. They fail to identify situations where job aids and templates would facilitate people becoming proficient faster, reduce variance across performers, and improve efficiency.

6. They do not make use of industry standards to set performance criteria or develop job procedures.

Essentially, they fail to partner with the appropriate people to create rules, tools, guides, and standards that support higher productivity and shorten the time it takes to make people proficient.

JOB AIDS OR QUICK REFERENCE GUIDES Jobs are a conglomerate of little tasks. Some of those tasks are done hourly or daily. Others are done less frequently, perhaps monthly, quarterly, semiannually, or annually. Some tasks, no matter how frequently they are done, must be done without error, for example, operate an airplane or a nuclear power plant or disassemble a high voltage transformer. Other tasks may require less precision but can consume too much time and materials when not done efficiently. In each of these cases, people can benefit from tools to help them be exact and efficient by reminding them of all of the rules, steps, and factors to consider.

Job aids are quick reference devices designed to direct or guide someone in the execution of a task. They contain information that prompts people to act in specific ways. Job aids are part of everyday life. For example, the pictures on the gasoline pump showing the sequence of how to purchase gas and fill your tank; the grocery list you create for yourself; the troubleshooting steps on the inside lid of the washing machine; and the instructions that come with a piece of equipment on how to assemble or install it. Job aids can be as simple as sticky notes attached to a computer or wall to remind you of information you might otherwise forget. They may use words, graphics, symbols, and colors; be electronic or in a printed format; and be permanently affixed to the site where they are needed or portable. The important thing is for them to be accessible when needed and that they use commonly understood symbols and terms.

When a task is dangerous or presents a lot of risk to people or assets (for example, landing an airplane) the use of job aids is required and built into the job; it is an expected way to do business. When the goal is to prevent errors, organizations seek ways to automate the task or design systems that limit people's decisions and prescribe a sequence of steps, like computerized data entry screens that only accept alpha or numeric symbols of predetermined lengths. Despite the growing use of electronic aids to guide people's decisions, job aids are still underutilized as tools to help people be more exact and efficient.

Types of Job Aids

Job aids usually come in one of seven formats, (1) worksheets, (2) arrays of information, (3) if, then decision tables, (4) flow charts, (5) checklists, (6) decision guides, and (7) templates.

1. Worksheets. These present a sequence of steps (usually a preferred path) and require you to respond in some way, such as by calculating math, adding dimensions, or filling in data. People who estimate the cost of jobs or the amount of materials that might be required frequently use worksheets. Worksheets are helpful when the task involves a sequence of steps, there is one path, and the person is to add data so a calculation can occur. An everyday example is the worksheet on the monthly bank statement showing you how to balance your checkbook, as shown in Figure 6.2.

**Figure 6.2. Sample
Worksheet: How to
Balance Your Checkbook**

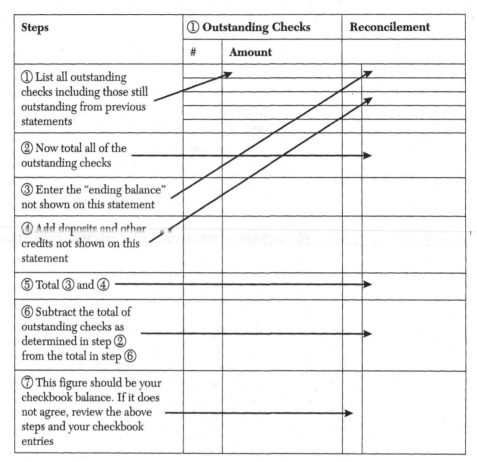

Figure 6.2. Sample Worksheet: How to Balance Your Checkbook

Steps	① Outstanding Checks		Reconcilement
	#	Amount	
① List all outstanding checks including those still outstanding from previous statements			
② Now total all of the outstanding checks			
③ Enter the "ending balance" not shown on this statement			
④ Add deposits and other credits not shown on this statement			
⑤ Total ③ and ④			
⑥ Subtract the total of outstanding checks as determined in step ② from the total in step ⑥			
⑦ This figure should be your checkbook balance. If it does not agree, review the above steps and your checkbook entries			

2. Arrays. These are directories or lists of data usually organized in some way, alphabetically, by size, age, or dimension, frequency of use, volume or application, and so forth (see Figure 6.3). Some examples are the phone book, a list of area codes, and product manuals with parts and model numbers. There is usually no starting point, no sequence of steps, but the data is organized in some meaningful way so you can choose where to start to best find the information you want.

3. If, Then Decision Tables. These tables present an "if, then" situation (see Figure 6.4). They guide you through a decision based on a set of conditions. An example is a table that helps you choose from a list of benefits (scope of health coverage, amount of the deductible, tax deductible funds for child care and transportation) based on your specific situation. The decision table helps you think through several variables; however, the number of choices is limited.

Figure 6.3. Sample Array: Candy Box Lid

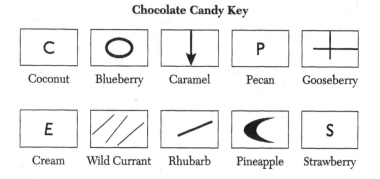

Chocolate Candy Key

Coconut   Blueberry   Caramel   Pecan   Gooseberry

Cream   Wild Currant   Rhubarb   Pineapple   Strawberry

Figure 6.4. Sample If, Then Decision Table: How to Clean Exterior Surfaces

If the surface is:	Then do this to clean it:
Heavily rusted steel	Use a power washer to blast clean the surface
Lightly rusted steel	Use a power washer to blast clean the surface or use a hand tool method
Covered with grease and oil	Wash the surface with a detergent and solvent
Covered with road salt	Wash the surface with a detergent and steam
Galvanized metal	Use a power washer to blast clean the surface
Covered with acid residue	Use a power washer to blast clean the surface
Covered with alkaline residue	Use an acid-etch cleaning method

Sales people frequently use decision tables to help customers decide on the most appropriate product or service, given their specific requirements.

4. Flow Charts. These graphically depict a sequence of tasks or decisions with decision points scattered throughout (see Figure 6.5). Flow charts are useful when the task involves a series of binary (yes/no) decisions and a clear path to a solution exists. An example is a chart that shows the information to be confirmed and the decision points that lead up to a larger decision such as whether or not to completely outsource a task or service, bring in temporary workers, hire more help, or rely on overtime work to finish a job.

5. Checklists. Checklists walk you through a procedure (see Figure 6.6). They are intended to help you remember every step when completeness or sequence is important. They are effective when you are faced with a complex task and you want to be sure to cover all of the steps. A checklist guide is especially helpful to less experienced workers because it can prevent mistakes and the omission of important steps.

Figure 6.5. Sample Flow Chart: Starting a Task

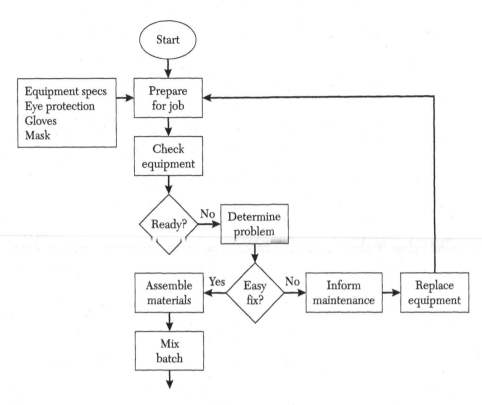

6. Decision Guides. These help you to think about a task or situation in a specific way. They are intended to prompt thinking. They are effective when you are faced with a moderately complex task and you want to be sure to consider a number of variables. A decision guide is especially helpful to less experienced workers because it can capture the factors considered and weighed by more experienced workers. Decision guides usually do not depict a sequence of steps, nor do they lead you to a clear solution. Instead, they help you remember what to think about and consider when faced with a decision. Most of the job aids in this book are decision guides (see Tool 6.1).

7. Templates. Templates are patterns, molds, preset forms, and default settings that help people be more productive and perform consistently. Examples are the patterns used in dressmaking and dyes used in the manufacturing of parts like automobile fenders and doors. In office settings, templates are frequently embedded in the word processing and presentation software. Similar to the other types of job aids, they guide actions and responses. They can also make it easier for customers and users to know how to respond. They are created to save time, to speed up the replication of parts used in manufacturing,

Figure 6.6. Sample Checklist: Air Sampler Maintenance Checklist

Step	Check if done	Comments
1. Disconnect the vacuum hose		
2. Connect new unit		
3. Check vacuum gauge; the reading should be at least 10 mm (millimeters of mercury)		
4. Take used unit to work station and record time on documentation form		
5. Remove nuts and lift off stage 0		
6. Lift out stage 0 petri dish		
7. Inspect medium for visible PM • Check for the pattern of the stage 0 holes in the medium • If no pattern, report finding to QC supervisor • Set aside		
8. Lift off stage 1		
9. Remove stage 1 petri dish (plate)		
10. Write date and time on dot stickers and label each dish • Set aside for transport to the QC lab		
11. Clean sampler with alcohol wipe		
12. Unwrap and inspect sterile petri dish for any visible PM and growth		
13. Set new dish on base plate		
14. Line up stage 1 holes with locator pins and set on dish		
15. Unwrap and inspect sterile petri dish for any visible PM or growth		
16. Put new dish on stage 1		
17. Line up stage 0 holes with locator pins and set on dish		
18. Put three retaining nuts on pins and tighten		
19. Document change		

and to reinforce an identity or image. Templates used in the creation of information, such as product and training manuals, save time both for the people who develop the manuals and for the people who use the information. The recipient, recognizing the template, knows how to maneuver through the information more quickly and how to respond appropriately. For example, the bill from the utility has the same look every month; only the amount due changes. The long example at the end of Chapter 4 on how to identify behaviors is an example of a template. You only need to overwrite the content and you have a description of behaviors by job level and level of proficiency.

The following guidelines are meant to help you identify opportunities to make better use of job aids.

TOOL 6.1: HOW TO SELECT AND USE JOB AIDS

Purpose
These guidelines are designed to help you identify those tasks that would most benefit from job aids and choose the type of job aid to use.

How
Together with your people, and perhaps a subject-matter expert, instructional designer, industrial engineer, technical writer, or graphic artist:

A. List the tasks that:

1. Are done infrequently (for example, complete the annual appraisal forms or produce an annual directory)

2. Are complex or require making fine discriminations (complete a tax form or interpret alarm conditions)

3. Involve a lot of steps that have to be done in sequence (dismantle a complex piece of equipment to perform maintenance or replace parts)

4. Have a high consequence of error (mislabel toxic materials, failure to maintain aseptic conditions)

5. Rely on people using knowledge that changes frequently (government regulations, new product features due to updates) or operate or service a large number of pieces of equipment

6. Take an excessive amount of time or overly involve a lot of people (multiple approvals or checking the effect of a change on other products or systems)

7. Are done by people in positions with high turnover (retail clerks, workers in fast-food restaurants, telemarketers)

8. Are redundant or require a lot of set-up time (periodic reports, manuals, presentation materials)

B. Identify those that would benefit from one or more job aids and say why (reduced rework, reduced error, save time, enhanced credibility, opportunity to standardize procedures, avoid set-up time, and so forth). Ask yourself what you want to be different as a result of people having job aids to help them do their jobs better.

C. Decide on the type of information the job aid should provide:

1. Some degree of calculation, as on a worksheet (figure the amount of materials, hours, costs, size, and so forth)

2. List of steps in a sequence, as a flow chart (first you . . . , then you . . . , then you . . . , and so forth)

3. A list of organized information in an array (customer account codes or account change codes, chemical symbols, people or products)

4. Decision guidelines on a decision table (if x happens, then do y; but if m happens, then do n instead)

5. Things to consider, as a checklist (remember this fact, check out this status, be sure to include x if you want to do y)

6. A preset form or model for a repeated task by one or more people, as a template (annual reports, periodic presentations, user manuals)

D. Discuss where and how the job aid will be used.

1. Determine where the job aid will most likely be used, at a customer site, outside, at the desk, in a controlled environment, or wherever

2. Identify any constraints, such as it must be able to be sterilized, fit in a pocket, supported by the information technology department, resistant to inclement weather, waterproof, resistant to acids

3. Identify any requirements, such as must have electricity, light, available wireless signal, printing capability

4. Identify any best practices, such as forms that are easy to use and produce the fewest errors

E. Meet with people who do the task well and ask them (perhaps with the help of a trainer, technical writer, or graphic artist) to create a prototype of the job aid you decided on.

F. Give the job aid to people who are less skilled at the task and ask them to try it out. Pay attention to the questions they ask, as this is an indication of unclear directions, missing steps, or lack of familiarity with the symbols or terms used.

G. Modify the job aid and ask people to use it again. Come back later to see whether it is working and reaping the benefits you expected.

Hint: Ease of use is very important. Job aids should not be cumbersome, heavy, or awkward. The goal is to get people to use them.

HOSPITAL OPERATING ROOM[1]

The hospital's accounting department reported an increase in incidents where patients were not billed for materials, supplies, or drugs used during their operations. The incident that triggered the need to look at the problem more seriously was the discovery that a patient was not charged for his pacemaker. Costs that should have been billed to a patient but were not became part of the hospital's basic operating room charge. After a little investigation, here is what was discovered.

- The one-page worksheet used to record what was consumed (materials, supplies, and drugs) during a surgical procedure was a standard size sheet of paper (8 1/2 × 11) and difficult to read because of the very small type. On the paper was a very long list of possible items, such as sutures, plasma, cotton swabs, anesthesia, and more. Beside each item was a little square for the nurse to check off whether an item was used. There were no instructions on how to indicate the quantity used, or how to indicate the type or model of item used. For example, sutures are made of different materials and some cost over $7 apiece and others are considerably less expensive, costing about 37 cents each. There were four lines at the bottom of the form to write in any materials not on the list. The result was that 85 percent of the items had to be written in, and these made up 60 percent of all of the chargeable items.

- The circulating nurse was responsible for recording all materials, supplies, and drugs used during each surgery, whether they were billable or not; however, no specific time was set aside to fill out the worksheet. Therefore, the nurses did it during their breaks or while the patients were in recovery.

- The nurses had developed their own coding system to note what item was used and how many, for example a check mark meant the item was used and a dot (·) represented the number used (prior to laser surgery a surgical procedure averaged sixty sutures so the nurse would regularly put in sixty or more dots). The accounting department did not understand the coding and only charged the patient for billable items with a checkmark.

- The nurses had never been told the value of the items or which items were part of the basic operating room charges and which were separate billable items.

The solution was a cooperative effort among accounting, nursing, and training. They did the following:

- Distinguished which materials, supplies, and drugs were to be billed separately and which were part of the basic OR charges.

- Redesigned the worksheet and clarified the symbols to be used. The first round produced a three-page worksheet that contained 100 percent of the billable items. However, the nurses felt it was too long and cumbersome. The second round produced a one-page worksheet with the thirty-seven most frequently used items, with the items of greatest dollar value graphically emphasized. For example, sutures made up 20 percent of the revenues, pacemakers 10 percent, and saline irrigations 10 percent.

- Recognized the importance of properly recording by setting a specific time for it to be done. A protocol was set up with the surgeons that at the beginning of the sponge count, the circulating nurse began filling out the worksheet.

- Informed the nurses of the dollar values of materials, supplies, and drugs and the cost implications of inadequate record keeping.

The result was that revenues from billable OR charges increased on average about $40,000 per month. Today, in addition to better job aids and working protocols, hospitals are implementing system solutions like bar coding and automated dispensing machines.

The operating room example is important because it shows a cooperative effort to diagnose and solve the problem. It would have been easy to just blame the nurses for not being more thorough. However, the problem, like many situations, required more than one solution. The worksheet was important, but so was the protocol with the surgeon, clarifying which items are billable, and telling people how much items cost.

OIL CHANGE[2]

One of the tasks on the production line was to replace the oil used to lubricate the machines. Barry, the supervisor, complained that workers either waited too long to replace the oil or replaced it too frequently. Dirty oil caused the machines to overheat. Replacing clean oil with clean oil added unnecessary costs. He could look at the oil and tell when it needed to be left alone, have clean oil added, or be completely replaced. But he also came to understand that his workers could not tell the difference. His solution was to arrange for three photographs. The first was a picture of clean oil next to the words "do nothing." The second was a picture of moderately dirty oil next to the words "add an equal amount of clean oil." The third was a picture of very dirty oil next to the words "dispose if it properly and replace" (see Figure 6.7). He had the pictures and words mounted on the same page, laminated the page, and hung it next to the machines.

Figure 6.7. Dirty Oil

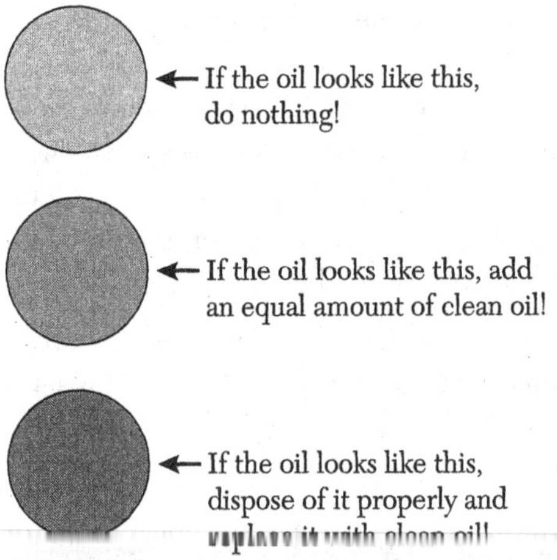

← If the oil looks like this, do nothing!

← If the oil looks like this, add an equal amount of clean oil!

← If the oil looks like this, dispose of it properly and replace it with clean oil!

ESTIMATING THE AREA OF A ROOF

A nationwide hardware firm offered home improvement among its products and services. One service was replacing roofs on homes. The sale involved estimating the area of a roof to calculate the amount of roofing required for the job. The salesmen used a worksheet on their handheld computers that walked them through a series of calculations. The worksheet included questions about the age of the current roof, type of roof, and how many roofs were already on the house. There were pictures of the four common roof types (hip and ridge, gable, mansard, and gambrel) so the salesmen only had to check the type that most resembled the customer's roof. The worksheet also walked the salesmen through the process of estimating the overall area of the roof. Insurance regulations prohibited salesmen from climbing on the roof to get dimensions. Instead, the salesmen had to pace off the width and length of the home. The challenge was how to factor in dormers and the added area due to the rise or pitch (steepness or slope) of the roof. To find the added dimensions caused by dormers, the salesmen simply counted shingles. To estimate the rise, they used a little pitch card (a laminated card that would fit in a shirt pocket) (see Figure 6.8). The pitch card had six angles that matched the six most common roof slopes.

On the reverse side of the card were the following instructions:

1. Stand about 50 feet from the center of the building.

2. Hold the card in one hand in front of you at eye level with your arm straight.

Figure 6.8. Pitch Card

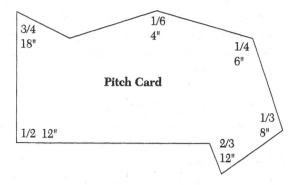

3. Raise the card so one of its tips is at the peak of the roof.

   • For gable roofs hold the card in a vertical position.

   • For hip roofs, slant the card toward the building to coincide exactly with the slant of the roof.

4. Turn the card to the different rises until its sides coincide with the slope of the roof.

A lot of jobs are made up of periodic tasks. Some tasks have higher risk associated with them, such as damaged relations; but a risk that is often overlooked is the excessive amount of time consumed compared to the value gained. Just as people did in the stories in this chapter, you and your people should identify the tasks that consume an excess amount of time and invest the time to create job aids, standards, and templates to make them easier and less time-consuming.

STANDARDS, WORK RULES, AND PROCEDURES

Three other resources in addition to job aids can help improve performance, bring people to proficiency faster, reduce errors, and smooth relationships with others. They are standards, work rules, and job procedures.

Standards

Standards are criteria used to judge adequacy, accuracy, speed, sufficiency, and the like. Standards tell you what should be. Industry standards consist of criteria adopted by specific industries. For example, the automotive repair industry has standards. The International Standards Organization (ISO) and the American National Standards Institute (ANSI) list standards.[3] The businesses that manufacture and maintain heating, air conditioning, and ventilation systems have standards. The State of Illinois has engaged in an aggressive effort to develop standards for jobs that are expected to be in demand in the future. The standards are designed for community colleges and trade schools to use to assure their training programs develop the skills required of employers. They are used by businesses to help them in the process of selecting and developing their own workforce.[4]

Similar to competency descriptions, standards come in different levels of detail. Some only contain statements about what should be. Others are very prescriptive and contain detailed procedures on how to execute a task and include the criteria for evaluating proficiency and productivity. Some, like those developed by the State of Illinois, have sufficient detail to support the creation of training materials and tests.

Some organizations misunderstand the difference between a *standard* and a *commonly accepted practice*. The difference is usually the degree to which the information is documented. Whenever standards are used, they should be relevant to the job.

Standards apply to more than people's performance or product specifications. They also apply to the design of information, reports, and other types of communication and to administrative tasks. In this case, the standards provide rules about when and how to use the company logo and what the official typeface, font, margins, and report layout are. Standards may also dictate when and what type of graphics to use. Standards can apply to job procedures, tools, and equipment, as they can dictate under what circumstances specific procedures, tools, or equipment should be used.

Work Rules

Work rules are put in place to assure consistency across people, shifts, and offices. Some work rules are officially negotiated between an organization and a labor union. Others just evolve from best practice. Work rules usually spell out the expected behaviors under normal conditions and may include what to do in the case of unusual circumstances. Work rules deal with who can make decisions, who can speak on behalf of the organization, and who has the authority to commit resources, including time, dollars, tools, and space. They are especially helpful at clarifying roles, responsibilities, and relationships with co-workers and other departments.

Procedures

Procedures usually explain the steps for doing a task. They are especially helpful for new hires or for tasks that are done infrequently. Some procedures are accompanied by job aids, specifically checklists and diagrams. An example is how to perform the Heimlich maneuver when someone is choking and cannot breathe. Other examples include the procedures for equipment set-up, operation, maintenance, and troubleshooting.

Job aids, standards, work rules, and procedures are most helpful for the following goals:

- To assure the safe execution of a task
- To assure the completeness or accuracy of a task
- To clarify roles, relationships, and responsibilities across work units and teams
- To eliminate redundant activity or rework
- To preserve, protect, and reinforce a brand image
- To facilitate or make reading and interpreting information easier
- To reduce costs by streamlining how work is done
- To reduce misinterpretation and errors

Here are guidelines on how to make better use of standards, work rules, and procedures.

TOOL 6.2: HOW TO IDENTIFY AND USE STANDARDS, WORK RULES, AND PROCEDURES

Purpose

These guidelines are designed to help you identify those tasks that would most benefit from standards, work rules, or procedures.

How

Together with your people, and perhaps an instructional designer, technical writer, or graphic artist:

A. Identify where standards, work rules, or procedures currently exist and incorporate them into the new hire orientation or on-the-job training as appropriate.

B. Identify why each was created, specifically the problems they are intended to solve or prevent.

C. Ask whether the solution (standard, work rule, or procedure) is still appropriate or whether it should be refined or replaced because of how work is currently done.

D. Identify the tasks where standards, work rules, or procedures do not exist, as evidenced by a lack of common criteria for judging the quality of work, materials having their own look, people complaining about others doing things out of turn, or unproductive time spent on figuring out how to do things or creating new procedures or formats.

1. Put the list in some order of priority, as in the frequency of the task, the time required, the amount of time wasted due to redundant activity or rework, how frequent the opportunity is for error, and so forth.

2. Decide on what you would like to be different, consider how much work is done, the quality of the work, customer ease or acceptance, and relationships with other departments.

3. Identify those opportunities where standards, rules, and procedures might save time and make life easier for employees, customers, co-workers, and others in the organization.

E. If the potential gain in productivity is significant, ask human resources or quality to put together a taskforce to create the standards, rules, or procedures. Be sure to try them out to see whether they save time, reduce errors, improve relationships, standardize the look, or accomplish what you think is important.

Hint: Be careful. Do not impose standards, work rules, or procedures without involving the people who will use them or be affected by them. Some people's joy in doing their jobs is in creating unique looks and doing their own thing. They might find standards and rules restrictive. If this is the case, build your argument for change on the basis that they make it easier for customers and improve accuracy.

THE ANNUAL MEMBERSHIP DIRECTORY

Mary worked for the director of membership of a major professional association. One of her tasks was to create an annual directory of the top two hundred most influential members of the association. Having one's name in the directory was a recognition that one had "arrived" in the eyes of peers.

The directory was to include the member's name, committee assignment, employer, work address, phone and email contact information, spouse's name, home address, and home phone and email address. The directory was published every November and sent only to those whose names appeared in it.

Mary's problem was keeping up-to-date on who should be added or deleted and finding accurate personal information, especially the spouse's name. It seemed this particular group of members divorced, remarried, and moved quite frequently. Publishing was one of many "little" assignments Mary had and she frequently held off doing anything until the last minute. As a result, the directory would go out with incorrect names of spouses and addresses, which in turn led to emotional outcries by the affected members. Because of the errors and the time it took to put out the directory, Mary and her boss decided to create a job aid and some templates. They decided they would know that the job aid and template worked if the directory came out on time, the time it took to do it met the boss's expectation, and there were no outcries by members about errors.

First, they created a flow chart, starting with the date the directory had to go to the publisher to be mailed on time. Working backwards, they identified all of things that had to happen, including the information that had to be assembled and corrected to go into the final product. Next, Mary created templates for the standard announcements about the directory, requests for current information, and for the layout of the directory. Finally, using her computer system, she created some reminders for herself about when to find out committee assignments, send out the requests, lay out the directory, proofread, and so forth.

PRODUCT MANUALS

Phyllis' department produces manuals to support the installation, operation, maintenance, and repair of the company's product line. Technical writers, graphic artists, and translators work for her. They take information from product development and create the manuals in seven different languages. The manuals come in two formats, a spiralbound version and a CD. Both versions are distributed to over 120 countries.

Phyllis' staff constantly complained that product development never gave them the information they required for the manuals. Phyllis complained more often about production costs. Phyllis decided to put together a task force that included a technical writer, graphic designer, translator, product specialist, and customer service representative to study the problem. The task force's charter was to come up with recommendations on how to shorten the cycle time for producing the manuals by eliminating delays and rework and to reduce development and production costs. The task force came up with the following suggestions:

- Create a template for product development that asked for the information required to do all aspects of a manual. The template could be electronic and cue the product developer to answer a series of questions the technical writer would have asked them normally. The task force stressed the importance of getting product development's involvement in the design. They believed a template would reduce the time it took to obtain the required information and better assure the accuracy of the information. Putting the template online would allow the product developers to complete it at their own pace, knowing it had to be complete by a specific date.

- Adopt a set of standards for the look and layout of the manuals, thus reducing the time spent on design. The standards could include if, when, and where to use photographs, line drawings, and inserts. It could address the required information versus the "nice to know." The task force believed standards would reduce the time and cost of design.

- Adopt a common lexicon or dictionary of terms. The task force believed that if the writers used language in a consistent way it would make translation easier, reduce the errors of users for whom English was a second language, and reduce writing time.

Phyllis was able to reduce costs and cycle time significantly. Customer service also reported fewer calls from people who did not understand the information in the manuals.

FIRST TO MARKET

Duane managed the documentation department for a pharmaceutical firm. His department maintained all the documents related to the testing of new drugs. He also helped the scientists prepare the documents that were sent to the Food and Drug Administration (FDA) requesting authorization to sell new products. Top management constantly complained that delays in getting FDA approval frequently lost the company the opportunity to be first to market with new drugs. Duane was asked to fix the problem.

Duane and two of his staff reviewed documents submitted over the past year and paid particular attention to the reasons for denial. The team discovered that every scientist had his or her own way of documenting the information the FDA wanted. Most of the refusals by the FDA were based on the fact that a document was missing key information. The team also discovered the information was frequently in the document, but rarely in the same place or noted in the same way. They also studied the documents that were accepted on the first submission. They learned that these documents were organized in the same way and used the same headings to emphasis specific information. The team came to the decision that many denials could have been prevented if the information were presented in a standard format. They took their findings to the scientists with the following recommendations:

- Adopt and follow a consistent standard for seeking FDA approval, including how the content is organized and sequenced and how and what headers are used

- Give the scientists a template in the organization's word processing software that would follow the standard

- Duane's group would continue to act as editors and help the scientist with the new format

The result was a significant drop in the number of denials by the FDA and more success in being first to market.

THE KEY[5]

The plant manager could not understand why the production levels of the second and third shift varied so much. It seemed that on some days little or nothing was done and on other days production was on schedule. He decided to find out why. He learned that the second and third shifts were fine as long as there were no equipment jams. It seemed that the manual to troubleshoot equipment problems was kept in the first-shift supervisor's office, which was locked when he went home for the day. If a later shift needed the manual, someone called him and he drove back to the plant to retrieve the manual.

Over the years the unstated rule was that the supervisor kept all equipment manuals in a locked office. This may have made sense at the time, but no longer. The adding of shifts to handle increases in production and the increased sophistication of the equipment made access to the manuals essential.

A lot of jobs are made up of periodic tasks. Some tasks have higher risk associated with them, such as damaged relations; but a risk that is often overlooked is the excessive amount of time consumed compared to the value gained. Just like in the stories in this chapter, you and your people should identify the tasks that consume an excess amount of time and invest the time to create job aids, standards, work rules, and procedures to make them easier and less time-consuming.

TIPS

Here are some suggestions on how to better equip your people so they are more productive and become proficient faster.

1. Be more aggressive when it comes to identifying or insisting on job aids and standards. These tools do not reduce creativity, but channel it in ways that add value to the organization. Great artists are very disciplined. They direct their talent to perfecting execution. Demand the same of your people.

2. Take the time to learn more about how work rules and procedures were developed and challenge their relevance today.

3. Adopt job aids, standards, work rules, and procedures to reduce the administrative trivia in your own job. Use them to help you be a more effective boss.

SUMMARY

People deserve the information and tools required to perform. To give people what they require, managers and supervisors have to challenge what the work rules are, why they were created, and whether they are still appropriate today. In addition to training, managers and supervisors should aggressively look for opportunities to make better use of job aids, standards, and templates to help their people become proficient faster. Capable people with the right support tools are more efficient and effective.

WHERE TO LEARN MORE

Here are some quick, easy books with useful information you can apply.

Rossett, A., and Gautier-Downes, J. *A Handbook of Job Aids* (San Francisco, CA: Pfeiffer, 1994).

Smith, P., and Kearny, L. *Creating Workplaces Where People Can Think* (San Francisco, CA: Jossey-Bass, 1994). A very nice paperback full of examples and directions on how to implement the ideas. About 200 pages.

NOTES

1. This story is based on the work of Greg Finnegan, director of organizational development, Johns Hopkins University Hospital, when he worked at Our Little Company of Mary Hospital in Chicago. He can be reached at gfinneg@jhmi.edu.

2. This story is based on the work of Barry Boothe, now retired, a champion of job aids when he was the training manager at Caterpillar Company, Joliet, Illinois.

3. ANSI now has available standards for the evaluation and qualification of personnel. They are the ISO/IEC 17024 *General Requirements for Bodies Operating Certification Systems of Persons.* You can find the standards at www.ansi.org.

4. The standards developed by the State of Illinois for over one hundred occupations can be found at www.standards.siu.edu. The standards include numerous jobs

within the following industries: healthcare and social services, hotel and hospitality, manufacturing, transportation, business and administrative, financial services, agriculture, natural resources, marketing, and retail. New standards are being developed continuously and those that are currently available are being updated to reflect new developments in science, technology, and customer requirements.

5. This story is based on the work of Barry Boothe when he worked with Caterpillar to identify barriers to performance.

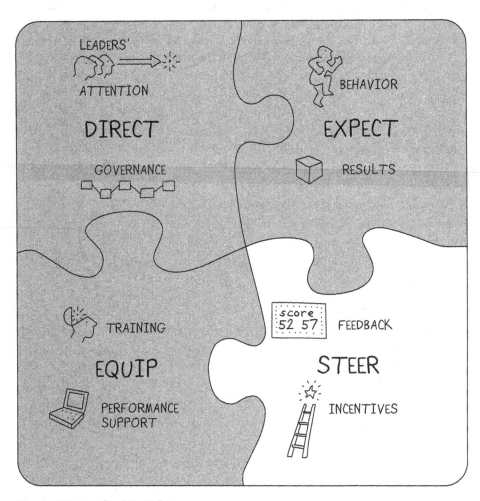

Figure 7.1. Leadership Roles

Lynn Kearny, CPT, Graphic Recorder

Chapter 7

How to Make Giving Feedback Less Painful

So how am I doing?
How do I rate?

*T*his chapter is about alternative ways to let departments, teams, and individuals know how well they are meeting expectations. Generally, there are two ways organizations communicate how well people are performing, and both ways leave a lot to be desired. The first way relies on the manager and supervisor to give people feedback. The second way is through the performance appraisal process. The reason these methods are less than stellar is that managers and supervisors hate to give feedback, and the information that comes out of the performance appraisal system is too removed from people's day-to-day work for even people's accomplishments to be useful. The goals of this chapter are to show you how to make giving feedback less painful through the use of tools and describe how to work within the constraints of a performance appraisal system to improve people's performance.

PERFORMANCE IMPROVEMENT

From a performance improvement perspective, people require and deserve information on how well they are doing. Therefore, performance improvement makes use of tools, techniques, and systems that the manager or supervisor can use to support giving people feedback. The information should be timely, relevant, and useful. It should be specific enough for people to act on, as feedback plays an important role in helping people deliver the expected results.

Also, from a performance improvement perspective, people require and deserve information during the annual review that is supported by what they were told over the course of the year. The annual review should be a formality, not a surprise. However, organizations frequently use the annual review for purposes beyond feedback, such as promotions, merit raises, and salary decisions. Therefore, it is especially important that you be clear on what information is shared and what you want as an outcome of the process.

COMMON MISSTEPS

Here are some of the mistakes managers and supervisors make that add to the pain of giving feedback:

1. They avoid giving feedback on a regular and consistent basis but wait until the activity is painful for everyone.

2. They assume people know how they are doing and think silence is sufficient feedback.

3. They overlook the numerous daily or weekly opportunities to say they like what they see or to ask questions when they are in doubt.

4. They do not take the time to establish goals, identify measures, and seek opportunities for feedback with their people.

5. They confuse conclusions with feedback.

6. They forget that giving feedback is a major part of their job.

PERFORMANCE PROBLEMS

One dilemma supervisors and managers face is how to identify the cause of poor performance. Most deficiencies are due to a lack of information, measures, and tools to do the job. If the problem is a lack of motivation, people should be reminded of the importance of the job and of the consequences of not performing. The solution is a combination of giving constructive feedback (tell people what they are doing that is unacceptable), making sure they have the required information (tell them what they need to know), and explaining the consequences (tell them what will happen if they do or do not change). However, you must act on the consequences if performance does not improve. Human resources is especially interested in seeing proof that people have been told that what they are doing is inadequate and why. This means you must document what you said and when. The more time that passes, the longer people are allowed to perform at an unacceptable level because no one confronted them, the harder it will be to discipline them.

If people have done something adequately in the past, and later have difficulty, then the cause is probably not a lack of skills and knowledge. It may be that they do not remember specific steps. In this case people should be given job aids to help them recall the rules for doing the task, especially if it's a task that is done infrequently. If the person has never done the task, then the solution is usually some type of training.

FEEDBACK AND COACHING

Feedback is information about the past. It is the information people expect after they have done something to know whether what they did was adequate. It tells them whether they should proceed in the same manner. Feedback is information about how one performed *in comparison* with what was expected. However, feedback is effective only when it informs, when it guides people to behave in ways that lead to the desired results. Unfortunately, statements like "You're late," "You're over budget," "You lost the account," "You can't get along with people," or "You're not a team player" are really conclusions and do not provide sufficient information for people to know what to do differently. They do not communicate what was observed or what was used as the basis for comparison. The key is being specific about the behaviors, criteria, or results that led to your conclusion and what it is you want someone to continue doing, change, or stop doing.

Coaching is information about the future and is what people deserve before they set out to do something so they are more likely to do what is right and do it in the best way. Coaching is not criticism about what people did wrong or failed to do in the past, but is about what they should do as they undertake an assignment.

However, too often feedback is associated with giving people bad news and coaching is associated with trying to correct someone's behavior instead of encouraging new behaviors. Because feedback and coaching are so closely associated with something being wrong, managers and supervisors tend to avoid them. Instead, they rely on silence to communicate that all is well and hope people will figure out what is wrong or how to do what is right. Being asked to give feedback or coach often means to be the bearer of bad news.

Daniel Goleman, in his book *Emotional Intelligence,* stresses the importance of feedback, but he, too, associates it with negative criticism.[1]

"Feedback [is] people getting the information essential to keep their efforts on track. . . . feedback is the lifeblood of the organization—the exchange of information that lets people know if the job they are dong is going well or needs to be fine-tuned, upgraded, or redirected entirely. Without feedback people are in the dark; they have no idea how they stand with their boss, with their peers, on in terms of what is expected of them, and any problems will only get worse as time passes. . . . criticism is one of the most important tasks a manager has. Yet it's also one of the most dreaded and put off." (p. 151)

KEN'S STORY

Ken was hired because of his extensive experience and abilities. He was immediately put into the position of a senior staff consultant. The job required him to design and conduct studies for the company and make recommendations about how to improve work processes to reduce costs or shorten cycle time. He frequently partnered with his boss on major assignments. He and his boss would meet with senior managers from the departments they were doing the analyses for to report their findings and recommendations. After every meeting with the senior managers, Ken's boss would say something like "Stop in my office. I'd like to talk to you." The words made Ken's stomach sink and he experienced a feeling of dread. In his previous employment, those words meant his boss was displeased and was about to launch into a tirade about what Ken did wrong. However, Ken's new boss had a different message. She would open with, "Ken, thanks for backing me up in the meeting. You spoke up at the right moments and gave the information the client needed to hear. I like knowing I can rely on you to back me up." She would go on with specific examples of where he spoke up, what he said, and why that was beneficial. It took Ken a long time to overcome the dread associated with the words "Ken, let's talk."

It took Ken's boss a long time to learn the importance of taking a few moments to give people feedback at key points in a project or when something was completed. She thought that just giving people the goals and the expected date of delivery was enough. She believed that no news was good news. It took a while for her to understand that people also wanted confirmation that they were okay and on track. Had Ken done something she thought inappropriate, she would schedule a meeting with Ken before the next client presentation to discuss how he might avoid the same mistake or do something differently.

WHY WE GIVE FEEDBACK

It helps if you decide what you want to accomplish in giving people feedback, as feedback can be used for many purposes:

- To let people know they are on track—confirm that what they are doing and how they are doing it is fine and should be continued

- To develop or improve people's performance—let people know what to do less of, more of, or differently

- To correct performance—let people know that what they are doing or how they are doing it is inappropriate, insufficient, dangerous, or unacceptable and what the consequences will be if they continue

Whatever the answer, ask yourself:

- How will the information help the individual and the company?
- How will a change in the person's behavior help him or her and the company?
- How does the person's current behavior hurt him or her and the company?
- How will the information be received?

WHY GIVING FEEDBACK IS DIFFICULT

Two factors make giving feedback dreadful. One is not having thought through what you will pay attention to when you evaluate someone's performance, but waiting until you see something you do not like. This puts you in the awkward position of catch up or clean up. You can reduce the chances of this by being clear on what you expect and what the measures of performance are. Therefore, you should identify the performance measures or indicators you will pay attention to as early as possible and share that information with employees. The second factor that makes giving feedback dreadful is not having the right words easily available so that what you say achieves the results you want. You can ease this problem by constructing a collection of statements and having them on hand before you need them.

SYSTEM SOLUTIONS

In addition to having performance measures and competency statements, you can make giving feedback easier by making use of systems that give people information about how well they are performing automatically. Here are some examples:

- At call centers the average call times are flashed on large screens around the center. The problem is that individuals only see the collective average of the group so they do not know whether they individually are doing well or not. The other limitation is that the system focuses on speed, not accuracy, courtesy, or helpfulness. Yet the system does provide some information so the manager or supervisor need only supplement it.
- At the FedEx hub in Memphis, Tennessee, the managers know the number of packages arriving for that night and everyone knows the amount of time scheduled to unload and reload all of the planes. Managers even know whether a plane will arrive late, perhaps due to bad weather, as this will affect the overall turnaround time. The amount of information available and its level of precision help set realistic expectations. The clock starts running at a scheduled time and stops when the sorting of all packages is complete. Additional time may be added to adjust for late aircraft or for

mechanical problems in the hub. The clock is visible throughout the hub, so employees can see how much time remains before they should be finished with the sorting. Everyone knows how long it took to unload and re-load the packages compared to the time scheduled. Teams are assigned to specific planes. All packages receive multiple scans as they pass through the sort. If a package is sorted incorrectly, it can be traced back to an individual, based on the scan data. This information is supplied to management, who are responsible for passing it on to the employee. In this situation, the system lets each of the managers and people know how well everyone performed in terms of time and accuracy.

- At a distribution center, the previous day's production is posted on a big board for each person in the pick and pack area. This system lets the shift see what it did the previous day and what each person did as well. The board also shows the volume of work in the cue for the upcoming day. In this system, giving feedback is relatively painless, unless someone falls behind. Then the feedback is not "you're slow" but rather a conversation about what to do to be faster and the consequences if a person does not adopt the recommendations.

In each of these examples, the measures were quantity, speed, and accuracy.

Project Plans and Budgets

You can use tools to help you communicate your expectations, then compare the behaviors you observed and results achieved to what was expected. Ideally, you can leverage the tools that were used in doing the work. For example, the tools people use to execute plans, manage projects, develop products, or follow a process can also be used to monitor their own performance. The tools include *project plans, action plans, budgets, statistical process reports,* and *meeting management protocols.* However, for these tools to provide feedback, the people using them have to track and compare what was done and how it was done with what was planned. Unfortunately, plans and budgets are created at the beginning, but actual time and costs are rarely captured and compared to the original estimates. If they are tracked, it is done at the end of the project when it is too late to take corrective action to improve the results. How many resources were used (people, time, materials, and money) compared to what was estimated is valuable information, but not if it comes too late to act on.

Timely feedback lets the people responsible for estimating know whether they should improve the methods they use to scope out work. Knowing whether the estimates were high or low compared to what occurred is how you improve. Knowing the difference between planned and actual allows you to identify the circumstances and factors that inflated either the estimates or the end results. This information is feedback if people use it to guide them in estimating jobs in the future. It is information you can use to judge the adequacy of someone's performance so you will know whether you should use him or her in the same capacity in the future.

TOOL 7.1: HOW TO USE PROJECT PLANS AND ACTION PLANS FOR GIVING FEEDBACK

Purpose

Leverage project planning and management tools so they help identify and compare specific behaviors and results to what was expected and thus make giving feedback easier.

How

Together with your staff:

   A. Create a project plan that includes tasks, milestones, and time estimates. Assign resources to each task.

   B. Pay particular attention to tasks that, once completed, are inputs to other tasks.

   C. Identify the behaviors that can help assure each task is on track and what events or behaviors might interfere or prevent it from staying on track. Include the resources required to keep it on track, such as time, budget, access to people or systems, approvals, and so forth.

   D. Create an action plan for how the project plan will be updated so that people can see where they are compared to the plan. In the action plan include who will do what, by when, how, and how the results will be communicated and used.

   E. Determine when you will meet to discuss progress and the behaviors the group identified.

   F. At major milestones, identify the future work that is created, stopped, or modified as a result of having reached that milestone.

   G. Create an action plan for how you expect people to use and communicate the outcomes from having reached a milestone. In that action plan include the information that is to be communicated, who will do it, and how it will be done.

   H. Add a line on the project plan for discussing progress and resolving problems.

   I. Make sure the people assigned to update the plan have done so before the meetings.

Hint: The meetings need not be long, but it is important that they be frequent. Short, frequent meetings, once you know what is expected and what behaviors to watch for, make giving feedback easier.

Budgets

Budgets can also provide useful feedback; however, once they are built, people rarely see how expenses compare to what was planned. A person may approve an expense item, but he or she may not always see the cumulative effect on the overall budget. As a manager or supervisor, you can make sure people see running totals. You can also meet to discuss the work that has to be done, ask for different ways to accomplish it, and guide your people to make wiser decisions about how to best use budgeted dollars.

ADVERTISING CAMPAIGNS

Joyce works in the marketing department of an international restaurant chain. She works with its advertising agency to identify, create, and launch campaigns in conjunction with professional and intercollegiate sporting events like playoffs and championships and entertainment events like movies and television shows. Usually, these campaigns start about two years prior to an event. Each campaign begins with the concept stage, where all of the elements (print and electronic ads, toys, contests, and so on) are identified and the budget developed. Next is the design phase, during which artists develop and present their creative ideas and the specifications are finalized for everything required to do the campaign. Last is the production phase, when the visual, electronic, and print media are developed by writers, artists, silk screeners, and plastic dye makers.

Over the course of the first two phases, management is invited to meetings to review and approve decisions that will affect costs. However, not all managers attend the meetings, but sometimes show up months later and ask that changes be made to the concept, the colors, the layout, or even the elements. These last-minute changes result in significant cost overruns in the millions of dollars. It was always assumed that management understood the implications of their requests for changes; however, they complained when they saw the final budget after the money was already spent.

Since Joyce is evaluated on how well she meets deadlines and stays within budget, she and her manager worked together to identify ways to prevent cost overruns. One idea they came up with was to create a project plan that showed the key milestones and whose work was dependent on decisions at specific points. They wanted to show that within five days after a meeting a toy manufacturer had already begun the process of creating dyes, silk screeners were cutting screens, sets were being built, and so forth. They also developed some protocols for keeping management informed and obtaining the required approvals in a timely fashion. For example, when managers missed a meeting, Joyce should send them an email stating what decisions were made and giving them a limited amount of time to approve or override the decisions. She would also give them cost estimates if changes were made past a certain date. She asked the advertising agency to change its response to management's request of "Can you change (a color, layout, format)?" to not just "Yes" but "Yes, and here's the cost implication." In the past, the advertising agency never mentioned the implications of a change either on the budget or the timeline.

Joyce and her manager agreed to review the plan every month to identify any slippage and discuss what to do about it and how to prevent it in the future. Joyce's evaluation now includes how well she uses the plan and budget to identify slippage, communicate the implications, and obtain management's signoff on any cost overruns before they occur. Using these tools made the job of giving Joyce feedback much easier. Joyce either used the tools and protocols or not. If the tools did not work, she was expected to refine them or seek help from others about what else she might do to stay on budget and within the timeframe.

If you were Joyce's boss, there are other things you might coach her on as well. For example, you could show her how to develop agendas that state what the expected decisions are at each meeting. She could develop a little briefing for management that shows the relationship of changes to cost overruns. Tools like plans, budgets, and agenda give you something to talk about that is constructive. Messages like "You're late" or "You're over budget" are not helpful. However, talking about what got in the way of making an agenda or following up with management can be more constructive.

Meeting Management

Guidelines have been developed to help people run meetings more efficiently and effectively, but unfortunately they are not always used. However, having such guidelines can be very helpful when giving people feedback about why meetings went well or not. Simple guidelines like the following can be used:

- Set objectives for meetings—define the outputs before you begin
- Decide on your outcomes—be clear on what you want the participants to do after and as a result of the meeting
- Start and end on time
- Stick to the agenda
- Document points or issues more appropriate for another meeting and commit to following up by a specific date
- Ask people to focus their attention on the subject under discussion instead of having sidebar conversations
- Decide how the group will decide, whether to formally vote on issues or use consensus

• Ask members who are quiet during discussions what they think and whether they want to add something to the discussion to assure that everyone is engaged and all opinions are counted

TOOL 7.2: HOW TO USE MEETING GUIDELINES TO GIVE FEEDBACK

Purpose

To use meeting agendas and protocols to help identify specific behaviors and results and thus make giving feedback easier. If you have decided on a set of guidelines, you are in a position to know what behaviors to watch for and your people are in a better position to monitor their own behavior.

How

Together with your staff:

A. Create a performance checklist like the one in Figure 7.2 so people can monitor how well they conduct meetings and you are in agreement on

Figure 7.2. Meeting Management Checklist

Task	Y/N	Comments
Agenda sent in advance?		
Agenda items expressed as objectives or in outcome terms?		
Person followed the protocols: • Started on time • Ended on time • Confirm who was taking notes • Followed the agenda unless asked to change the order • Recorded issues for later discussion or referral to others		
Kept everyone engaged		
Accomplished the objectives of the meeting		
Asked people to report on accomplishments		
Created a post-meeting action plan • Who does what? • By when? • How?		
Other		

what behaviors are expected. You can delete, add, or modify the tasks on the checklist to meet your requirements.

B. At the end of each meeting, have the person complete the checklist.

C. If you participate or observe the meetings periodically, bring a copy of the checklist to capture your observations.

1. Add or modify the checklist to capture the behaviors and accomplishments you think are important

2. Meet with the person afterward to discuss your proposed changes to the checklist and your observations

3. Agree to meet periodically to discuss how well the person is managing the meetings

Hint: You can add competency statements related to communication and interpersonal skills to the checklist to reinforce the importance of those behaviors.

PROGRAM AND CONTRACT MANAGEMENT

Joe was the program manager for the implementation of a new computer system. It was expected to take three years for the system to be fully functional. This was an important assignment for Joe, and he was relieved of his other supervisory duties so he could dedicate all of his time to managing the implementation. Part of his job was to chair the meetings of the steering committee that were held twice a month. The steering committee was made up of managers from five different departments, including Joe's boss, Harry, and the consultant who built the computer system. The purpose of the meetings was to discuss progress, decide how to communicate with the departments affected by the new system, and resolve issues about how to best staff specific activities, such as mapping work processes, collecting, coding, and entering data into the new system.

At the last meeting that was held, Harry observed that the consultant, not Joe, ran the meeting. The consultant made additions to the agenda without asking the other members whether that was okay. When Mary, a member of the IT team, gave a report on what her team had done, the consultant disagreed with the team's actions and criticized Mary for the way the team was going about its assignment. When one of the steering committee members asked about another person's role on the project, the consultant announced that the person in question would never play a role. When one of the members of the steering committee started to challenge a point made, the consultant interrupted him, essentially cutting him off. The other members of the steering committee sat quietly, saying nothing.

After the meeting Harry asked to meet with Joe, saying, "Joe, I want to share my observations about the meeting with you. Do you have time this afternoon?" During their meeting, Harry shared his observations that the consultant, not Joe, ran the meeting, that the other members checked out, and that Mary was just reporting her team's decisions and it was not the appropriate place to challenge the decisions of her team. Harry then mentioned Joe's specific behaviors that caused him to lose control of the meeting, including that Joe did not speak up when the consultant wanted to change the agenda, he did not ask the members of the steering committee to confirm their acceptance of a change in the agenda or even the sequence of the items on the agenda, and he did not intervene on behalf of the member who was interrupted or ask that any criticism of Mary or her team be discussed with her team.

Harry then asked Joe what he might do to prevent this sort of situation from happening in the future. Together they decided to reinstitute some basic meeting management protocols, such as:

- Putting the agenda out ahead of time and asking members whether they had any additions

- Reviewing the agenda and objectives of the meeting at the beginning of the meeting

- Not allowing changes unless the members agreed to them

- Restating the purpose of team updates

- Not interrupting one another

- Periodically asking individual team members whether they had anything to add to a discussion, whether they agreed with the suggestions being made, and so forth

Harry went on to suggest that Joe sit where he could easily see everyone's faces and have direct eye contact with them. Joe volunteered to speak to the consultant and remind him that his role was that of an observer, not a participant in the meeting.

Harry then asked how the project was going according to schedule and budget. He discovered that Joe did not see the budget and had no idea where they stood. He was behind schedule according to the project plan, but this was because the budget had not been approved to train people in data collection. Harry agreed to arrange with purchasing for Joe to see what expenses had been approved, see what charges were made to the project, and obtain a copy of the budget. He also agreed to find out about funding for training.

This meeting may have been uncomfortable for Harry and Joe, but it was essential that Joe receive feedback about how his behavior, not just the consultant's behavior, was inappropriate given his new role and the importance of the project. It would have been easier for Harry to talk about the consultant's behavior, but the real problem was Joe's behavior. It would have been better for Harry and Joe to meet earlier in the project to define expectations and identify tools that Joe might use to help him in his new role.

Customer Surveys

The same tips apply to customers as apply to supervising people. The tools and techniques people can use to measure their own effectiveness include customer satisfaction surveys, frequent meetings with key customers, and debriefings at specific intervals to check how things are going. Follow up on what you learn and use the information to modify your behavior. You should also sit down with your people and identify factors that signal a customer relationship is not as you might like it to be. The indicators might be difficulty getting an appointment, calls not being returned, and appointments being canceled; unfortunately, these indicators tell you a relationship is already in trouble. If you meet frequently with customers, you are in a better position to learn in advance whether all is well. Look for the early warning signs so you can intervene before people are entrenched in their opinions.

Many organizations do customer surveys on a regular basis, but they are sent to external customers and the data may not be shared within the organization. If your organization conducts customer surveys, ask to see the data relevant to your group. You can also survey internal customers, but you should have more flexibility about how you do it. For example, you can talk to them on the phone or in person. You can send emails with a few questions. You can even ask them to participate in a focus group. Questions like "How satisfied are you with our service?" do not generate enough information to be helpful. Ask questions that get at specific behaviors. Here is a job aid to help you start.

TOOL 7.3: HOW TO OBTAIN AND USE INTERNAL CUSTOMER FEEDBACK

Purpose

The purpose is to obtain internal customer survey data to help give feedback to employees and reinforce specific behaviors.

How

You can do this with the help of your customer relations, quality assurance, or training departments. First use any survey data you already have. Ask whether the department that does the survey can separate out results about your people. If you do not survey your internal customers, develop a protocol to do so. You can survey people in person, on the phone, or by email. You can ask questions individually or in a group.

   A. Consider the following questions and, together with your people, add, delete, or modify them to best meet your requirements.

   1. What do you expect of my people?

   2. What do my people do that you most appreciate?

   3. What do my people do that you find least helpful?

   4. If my people could do three things better, what would they be?

   5. Is there anything my people should keep doing, no matter what?

   6. Think about an experience with my group (people, department) that you thought went especially well. What was it that made this particular experience positive?

   7. Think about an experience with my group (people, department) that you thought did not go well. What was it that made this particular experience fall short of your expectations?

   B. Together with your people, agree on the individuals or groups you will survey, who will do it, and when it will be done.

   C. Conduct the survey.

   D. Review the results with your people.

Hint: You may learn things that are beyond your control; however, you may find out something of value. Get in the habit of asking.

Intellectual Work

The tools you have available to provide ongoing feedback include industry or professional standards and peer reviews. You can wait until the end to see whether the work that was done accomplished the goal, but this might take months or years. If you put a process in place that incorporates comparing work to standards or sets up peer reviews, people are in a better position to incorporate what they learn and to improve. You are also in a better position to identify problems early and to be able to act on them.

Intellectual work is especially difficult because, even though acceptance is desired, it is not always what leads to breakthroughs or innovations. Therefore, the behaviors you might want to consider are how often people challenge each other's work, how they challenge it, and on what basis they consider or reject each other's comments.

It is easy to think of feedback in a clinical way as just the facts. The facts become information if they *compare* what people did and accomplished to some expectation or standard. However, people want more than facts; they deserve specifics about what it is you want changed. They also deserve an acknowledgement that you know what they are doing and how well they are doing it, and that you care. Feedback lets people know that you care about what they do. Just about everyone wants confirmation he or she was noticed and that what he or she does matters. The challenge is how to let people know they are on track without being reduced to only a trite phrase like, "You're doing great!"

ONLINE GRADUATE COURSE

Grace was asked to teach an online graduate course for a university. This was her first time teaching online. The seventeen students were from all over North America and worked full time for a variety of industries, including the military, utilities, healthcare, insurance, and banking. She would never meet her students in person. She would post the week's assignment with discussion questions on the university's database. The students were given passwords that allowed them to access the database from anywhere in the world.

At the beginning of the class, Grace posted how grades would be calculated and on what basis points would be assigned to the class project and the weekly discussion questions. She stated how many points each had to earn to receive an A, B, or a C. She thought that having a clear definition of what was expected, what the performance measures were, and how those measures were to be calculated would be enough information. She expected the students to take the information and track their own points for participation. Grace carefully monitored the weekly discussions and only responded when she saw a student misinterpret the text or if he or she posed a question to her.

Half-way through the course, Grace sent out a survey asking students for feedback. She discovered that the students wanted confirmation that she cared about them, knew them, and was interested in what they thought about the points being discussed. However, instead of asking, "Do you like me and are you impressed with what I had to say?" they asked for confirmation that they were earning the maximum number of points, information they could easily calculate for themselves. Her giving them the rules and the tools to calculate their own grade was insufficient. She knew from their discussions they were learning and she thought intervening just to keep them on track was enough; however, wanting acknowledgement is a human need and the next time she teaches she'll provide a running total of points for every student with specific comments on their insightfulness.

PERFORMANCE APPRAISALS AND FEEDBACK

Performance appraisals are one of the more disliked aspects of being a manager. Employees, too, find the process unrewarding. A reason they are ineffective is that people are unable to see the connection between what is talked about, what was expected, what was measured, and what they did. Yet performance appraisal systems are supposedly put in place to help you judge individual and team performance, help employees understand what is expected of them, and help the organization make compensation decisions. Performance appraisals are imposed by the organization for many reasons, among them:

- To assure that managers set and communicate annual goals with their people
- To align people's attention and work goals with the needs of the organization
- To measure how well people accomplished the goals
- To assure that people receive, at a minimum, annual feedback on how well they are doing

However, annual performance appraisals are not a substitute for feedback in terms of supporting performance, as the information people receive is too infrequent and removed from what they do over the course of a year. The performance appraisal system may even track factors that are different from what you consider to be important.

The annual review is not the event for people to hear for the first time that they are on track, need to improve their performance, or need to correct their performance. For performance appraisals to be effective:

- Managers and supervisors have to be held accountable for conducting the formal reviews, setting targets, polling constituents, giving feedback, and making adjustments as appropriate
- People have to believe the criteria used to evaluate them is fair and within their control
- More than one set of measures should be set for judging performance
- Managers should have the skills to communicate expectations, give feedback, and recognize the difference between adequate and deficient performance

Annual performance appraisals are done at the individual and team levels. Department and division performance are usually evaluated based on meeting long-term strategic goals. Investors evaluate the organization's performance by considering earnings, labor stability, growth potential, debt, and other things.

Other requirements that employees must meet include:

- Complying with organizational policies
- Complying with safety regulations
- Being at work during work hours and when scheduled (attendance and tardiness)
- Cooperating with co-workers, customers, and other business partners
- Complying with the dress codes
- Documenting work performed, exceptions, customer issues, and so on
- Demonstrating the competencies

Organizations have rules about what measures to consider during the annual performance appraisal. Whether or not those measures are appropriate depend on the organization's goals, the work unit's goals, and the individual's developmental needs. Some organizations dictate that every employee's performance measures should include at a minimum:

- The accomplishment of key objectives
- At least one developmental goal

Other organizations dictate measures that include some combination of the following:

- Team performance (goal accomplishment)
- Individual performance (meet quota or standard)
- Core competencies (leadership, communication)
- Technical or job-specific competencies (blueprint reading, machine operation, financial analysis)
- Productivity goals (volume and quality of outputs)
- Customer satisfaction (ratings, retention, cost of service or sales)
- Product performance (reliability, shelf life)
- Financial performance (cash flow, cost avoidance, cost reduction, revenues)

These other goals make it difficult to connect the information exchanged during annual performance appraisals to what seems important on the job.

Figure 7.3. Phenomena That Contribute to Unfair Evaluations

> **The bias of memory**
> There is a tendency to over-emphasize recent events and not consider a person's performance over the whole evaluation period. The problem is best prevented by:
> - Identifying the specific measurable indicators of performance at the beginning of the evaluation period
> - Giving feedback at more frequent intervals
>
> **The bias of association**
> Another phenomenon happens when you evaluate a very good or very poor employee and inadvertently compare a different employee with the first. The problem is best prevented by:
> - Collecting specific measures of performance before conducting the evaluation
> - Only using the criteria decided on at the beginning

Measures must be

- Relevant—reflect the actual job requirements
- Unbiased—be about performance-related factors, not personality
- Significant—relate to outcomes important to the organization
- Practical—capable of being accurately tracked or captured

Organizations would be better off if they required measures that could be monitored throughout the year and through managers' feedback or through checking one's own performance. Some specific phenomena that contribute to unfair evaluations are listed in Figure 7.3.

Many performance appraisals require you to rate people using some type of scale. A commonly used scale is shown in Figure 7.4.

Figure 7.4. Sample Rating Scale

Needs Improvement		Satisfactory		Exceeds Expectations
1	2	3	4	5

However, scales do not give you or your people sufficient information. They are inadequate as feedback unless you can cite the specific behaviors, outputs, or outcomes on which they are based. Therefore, identify specific quantitative descriptors for each point on the scale. Decide in advance what or how many incidents of behaviors, outputs, or outcomes would be necessary for each rating.

The guidelines that follow will help you give feedback to employees.

TOOL 7.4: GUIDELINES FOR GIVING FEEDBACK

Purpose

The purpose of this job aid is to help you prepare for those more formal feedback sessions, such as a project milestone or when a major deliverable is completed. These guidelines can also be used for an annual performance appraisal.

How

The guidelines include what to do before, during, and after a session.

    A. Before

1. Meet with your people individually to discuss the goals, measures, and any other requirements.

2. Together decide what behaviors and results you will monitor.

3. Identify any other factors that will be considered such as attendance, compliance with policies, safety, or teamwork.

4. Identify tools that will help each person monitor his or her own performance, such as project plans, budgets, meeting protocols, and customer surveys.

5. Before you meet with someone individually, decide what you want to accomplish by giving that person feedback. Is the purpose:

    a. To correct behavior? People deserve knowing where they are deficient, what criteria you are using, and what you will use as evidence that performance has improved.

    b. To improve performance? People deserve a clear set of expectations, measures, feedback, and what you will accept as evidence that performance has improved.

    c. To encourage continued performance? People deserve feedback and encouragement.

    d. To develop someone for a new or future role? People deserve coaching about how to do well and not embarrass themselves as they undertake new assignments.

6. Take into consideration the person's:

    a. Developmental stage—a new hire, a novice, moderately experienced, a consistent performer. The less developed the person, the more frequently feedback is needed.

    b. Past performance—satisfactory, exceeded expectations, fell short of expectations. The less acceptable past performance was, the greater the need for frequent feedback and agreement on what it is about the performance that is not meeting expectations.

7. Consider attributes of the job, such as:

   a. The consistency and complexity of the information, tools, materials, and other items the person has to work with (inputs). As the complexity of the job increases, focus the expectations and the feedback on the wise use of resources to help manage and possibly reduce the complexity.

   b. The degree to which the job's procedures and processes are well-defined. The more prescribed the work, the more important it is to focus expectations and feedback on complying with the procedures and being efficient in their execution. The less well-prescribed the work, the more important it is to focus your feedback on how people should develop or standardize processes and work protocols and perhaps solidify relationships.

   c. The expected quantity and quality of the outputs of the job. The more important it is that people's work meet a standard for quantity and quality, the more important it is for those standards to be easily available and used consistently to judge people's work.

8. Measure and obtain the facts. Consider the obvious (goal accomplishment) and the less obvious or hidden impact (the amount of supervisory time and energy it takes to either help the person achieve the goal or clean up after him or her).

9. Decide for yourself what behaviors you want your feedback to influence and what you will use as evidence that the behaviors are appropriate or inappropriate.

B. During

1. Tell the person why you are meeting and what you want to accomplish.

2. Tell the person what you observed in terms of behaviors, work being done, and so forth. Provide written examples if appropriate.

3. State what you want the person to continue doing, change the way he or she is doing it, or stop doing.

4. Allow time to exchange ideas.

5. Ask what it will take for the behavior to continue, change, or cease.

6. If your message is about stopping or changing and it is serious, state what the consequences will be if the person does not stop or change his or her behavior.

7. Together determine what tools or other resources could be used to help the person monitor his or her own performance.

8. Determine how both of you will use the tools, how frequently you will review the information gained from the tools, and what you will do with the information.

9. If the purpose is to correct a behavior or improve a performance, together agree on the specific measures (evidence you will want of improvement or change) and set up a time when you will meet again to discuss the results.

C. After

1. Meet your commitment to give feedback, whether weekly or at key milestones.

2. Make sure your people have access to and can use the tools that will help them monitor their own performance.

Hint: The better prepared you are, the easier it is to give people feedback. Remember, feedback is information they can act on.

Here are some suggestions to help you align the measures with the organization's goals.

1. Walk around. Be seen. Use every encounter to ask about work, projects, and accomplishments. If you have doubts about what someone is doing, ask:

- How is it going?
- How far have you gotten since the last time we spoke?
- What is getting in the way?
- Who are you working with?
- What do you need?

Paraphrase what you heard to confirm you understood.

2. If your feedback is about a recurring activity and people are not doing it to your expectation, frame your message so it is about what to do differently and how. Do not limit the message to what's wrong.

3. Develop a project plan for yourself as a planning and communication tool. When you put together the plan identify:

- What information you will gather or confirm so your comments can be specific
- When you will meet or communicate with specific people

4. Hold yourself accountable for carrying out the plan.

5. If the performance appraisal system is dysfunctional, keep your feedback sessions separate from it. When you do have an annual review, do not speak ill of the organization.

SUMMARY

Feedback requires you to have information relevant to what is expected and the communication skills to convey the information so that it is meaningful and helpful. The information required to give people feedback comes from:

- Goals—what is expected, what you want people to accomplish
- Performance measures—what evidence you will use to judge the adequacy of what the person did
- Competencies—what behaviors you expect to see because they will lead to accomplishments and constructive working relationships
- Comparisons—what you see as the difference between what was done and what was expected

If you are not clear on what you want people to accomplish and on what you will use as evidence of success, it is difficult if not impossible to give people meaningful feedback, no matter how good you are at communicating. Take advantage of tools that can help people monitor their own performance. The tools will help you direct your comments.

WHERE TO LEARN MORE

Try these books for more on the topic.

Daniels, W.R. *Breakthrough Performance: Managing for Speed and Flexibility* (Mill Valley, CA: ACT Publishing, 1995). Check out Chapter 8, as it has wonderful suggestions on running meetings and exercising power and Chapter 10, which is about giving advice and coaching.

Goleman, D. *Emotional Intelligence: Why It Can Matter More Than IQ* (New York: Bantam, 1997). This is a hefty paperback of over three hundred pages that is full of research and insights. If the whole book is too much, check out Chapter 3, "When Dumb Is Smart," on pages 33–45; Chapter 8, "The Social Arts," on pages 111–128; and Chapter 10, "Managing with Heart," pages 148–163.

Stolovitch, H.D., and Keeps, E.J. *The Handbook of Human Performance Technology: A Comprehensive Guide for Analyzing and Solving Performance Problems in Organizations* (Silver Spring, MD: International Society for Performance Improvement, 1992). This book can be daunting on first sight; however, Chapter 18 by William Deterline on Feedback Systems is well worth the time. If nothing else, check the book out of the library and read the seventeen pages on feedback. It is an easy and informative read.

Weiss, D.H. *Why Didn't I Say That?! What to Say and How to Say It in Tough Situations on the Job* (New York: American Management Association, 1994). A nice little paperback full of examples of what to say when and why, whether the goal is to give feedback or encouragement, coach, or reprimand. Check Chapter 7 on reviews and appraisals. There are examples of ideal and less than ideal situations. About two hundred pages.

NOTE

1. Goleman, D. *Emotional Intelligence* (New York: Bantam, 1998).

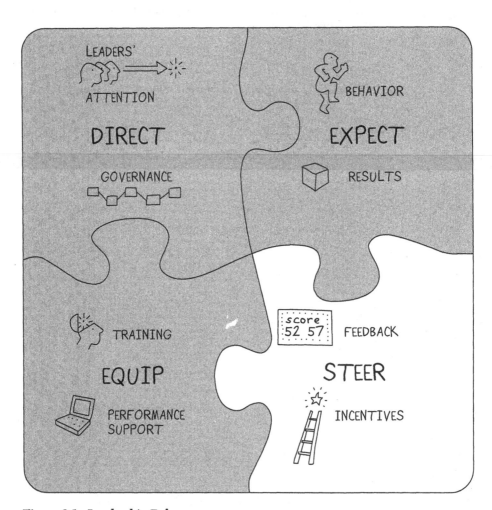

Figure 8.1. Leadership Roles

Lynn Kearny, CPT, Graphic Recorder

Chapter 8

How to Recognize and Reward People

Why should I try? What's in it for me? What's in it for you?

*T*his chapter continues with the idea that your job is to steer people, helping them stay the course and stay on course. Ongoing feedback is one way to steer; the use of incentives is another. You can think of incentives as a form of feedback, because they act as signals, they send cues about what is important to you and what you want people to do. The right incentives increase the odds that your people will perform to the level you expect. Therefore, this chapter is about how to select and use incentives to encourage the behaviors the business values and recognize and reward those people whose efforts produce results.

Incentives are promises of a reward. The promise is that good things will happen if people behave in certain ways, engage in specific activities, and achieve certain results. *Rewards* are how organizations fulfill the promise. *Recognition* is how the organization acknowledges and shows appreciation for people engaged in the desired behaviors and for the accomplishments that ensue. *Awards* are a type of recognition or reward that usually take the form of a certificate, a trophy, or a cash bonus. *Incentive plans* and *recognition plans* are programs organizations put in place to manage what behaviors and results are rewarded and how. These programs usually specify the criteria for using incentives and how rewards are earned.

> "Behavior change and measurable results derive from incentive plans. A feeling of appreciation and acknowledgment occurs with recognition."[1]

An incentive can be a promise of a future reward, such as a bonus based on some percentage of the organization's earnings at the end of the fiscal year. It can also be something that is given to encourage the continuation of specific behaviors or activities, like a catered lunch if a project is on schedule. Recognition

Figure 8.2. A Comparison of Incentives and Rewards

Factor	Incentive	Rewards
What it is	• A promise of a future reward • Something earned to encourage the continuation of or the achievement of specific results, behaviors, or activities	• Something given after the fact in appreciation of good work or acknowledgement of some result or achievement • Something given to encourage the continuation of specific behaviors or activities
When it occurs	Before, during, or after an activity, event, or result	Either during an activity, after a result, or after the fact
Purpose	• To encourage and motivate people to behave in specific ways or to achieve improved results • To provide direction	• To motivate when done during an activity • To acknowledge when done after the results are in
Criteria	• Tied to desired results • May be tied to behaviors that lead to results	Tied to desired results or specific behaviors that lead to results

Adapted from a table developed by Rodger Stotz, vice president and managing consultant, Maritz Inc.

programs may use financial rewards, like gift certificates or a company jacket, or non-financial awards, like a personal or public thank you, a memo in the personnel file, or a letter to upper management telling them about a person's work. Financial rewards, for example, money, trips, time off, or large gifts, are susceptible to being treated as taxable income. The words "incentives," "recognition," "rewards," and "awards" are used interchangeably in everyday conversation. However you use them, it is important to be clear about what you want to accomplish. Figure 8.2 shows some of the differences.

PERFORMANCE IMPROVEMENT

From a performance improvement perspective, the first question you should ask yourself is what you want to accomplish by using incentives or rewards. What is the result you want? The second question is how you will know whether the incentive or reward did what you wanted it to do. Performance improvement means following a systematic process to identify and use appropriate incentives to get the results you want.

Without a systematic process, you risk motivating the wrong behaviors and rewarding people whose work does not contribute to long-term success.

COMMON MISSTEPS

Here are some of the mistakes managers and supervisors make when they want to motivate people or recognize their accomplishments:

1. They fail to point out the importance of the work to be done.

2. They discount the significance of a personal thank you, general courtesies, and politeness.

3. They are unclear on their purpose—whether they want to encourage specific behaviors or reward results.

4. They fail to link the reward or recognition to performance.

5. They do not reward people fairly or equitably.

6. They think treating everyone the same is best.

7. They think treating everyone differently is best.

8. They reward meaningless results.

LEADING AND LAGGING INDICATORS

The presence of some activities and behaviors improves the odds that the organization will be successful. Some examples are (1) following up with customers in a timely fashion, (2) cleaning up after your work at a client's site, (3) being thorough in documenting what was done to prevent rework or errors, (4) complying with safety procedures, and (5) giving employees frequent feedback. Similarly, the absence of these or other behaviors or activities increases the risk the organization will not get the results it wants, for example, (1) failing to disclose a product's limitations, (2) not being honest about delivery dates, and (3) promising capability that cannot be carried through. These behaviors and activities are *"leading"* indicators, because their presence or absence correlates with producing results.

Accomplishments are *"lagging"* indicators, because they are the results that occurred after people engaged in specific activities and behaviors. They tell you whether what you assumed would produce results did or did not actually produce them. Some examples of lagging indicators are (1) the amount of product sold compared to quota, (2) the customer satisfaction rating received compared to what was expected, (3) the percent of market share attained compared to goal, (4) the number of accidents or lost time injuries that occurred compared to a previous time period, (5) the amount of costs reduced or avoided compared to plan, and (6) the quality of the work produced compared to what was promised. If you fail to encourage the behaviors that lead to results but wait until the results come in to recognize what people accomplished, you risk not getting the outcomes you want.

Some of the choices you have to make will be around whether to use incentives to encourage the behaviors and activities you believe will achieve the results or to wait until the results come in and reward those people who were successful. Since the goal is for everyone to succeed, not just some people, you might want to consider encouraging behaviors that are leading indicators, as this increases the odds that everyone will be successful. However, when the results fall short of what was expected, you should first revisit your assumptions about what it is that people do that leads to results and, second, question whether they had adequate direction and resources to do the work. Sometimes what people think leads to good results is wrong. Here are two examples.

CALL CENTER SALES
AND SERVICE REPS AT A FINANCIAL SERVICES FIRM

Call center reps answer customers' questions about their accounts, handle the sale and purchase of investments, and advise customers on investment options. Reps are evaluated on their average call handling time, call volume, and time between calls. They are rewarded on how much they exceed the average.

Management assumed a high level of call volume coupled with a low amount of time between calls equated to productivity and client satisfaction. However, they learned that the measures of talk time might be related to productivity, but not to client satisfaction. Measuring customer behavior was a better indication of satisfaction, for example, how many sales transactions a customer made and the overall value of the transactions.

Since reps work in teams that are assigned to customer types, the company can track customer behaviors and link them to specific teams. Therefore, it decided to reward reps based on their customers' behavior plus the average call handling times, volumes, and so forth.

FAR EXCEEDS

Union personnel were accustomed to receiving a rating of "far exceeds" on their annual performance reviews. In fact "far exceeds" was the norm. It was rare for anyone to not receive a "far exceeds." When the company put in a new performance management system with measures tied to the organization's five large goals, managers were told very few people should expect to receive a "far exceeds" on the annual review. Managers were encouraged instead to use the reward system to recognize employees who did good work but whose overall performance did not meet the "far exceeds" criteria. So this is what the managers and supervisors did. The result was that in one year, the company doubled the amount given out through the reward system. After studying what people did to earn the rewards, the company learned that managers were rewarding small rather than significant improvements where a genuine thank you would have been sufficient. The managers were using the reward system to make people happy, not to achieve performance.

LEADING INDICATORS

Results happen when managers, supervisors, and workers engage in specific behaviors and activities. Those behaviors and activities are *leading* indicators. Incentive plans can be designed to encourage the behaviors and activities that are linked to results.

Supervisory Behaviors

Some leading indicators of good employee relations and performance are supervisory behaviors such as:

- Setting clear expectations
- Giving regular and frequent feedback
- Regularly displaying common courtesies
- Saying thank you
- Being fair when giving people attention or help
- Explaining the organization's vision and his or her vision for the work unit
- Showing respect
- Taking an interest in people's careers

The challenge is finding and applying incentives that encourage managers and supervisors to incorporate these behaviors in their day-to-day transactions with people and recognizing them when they do. Here is an example.

HOUSEKEEPING SERVICES

Airlines contract with Housekeeping Services (HS) to clean their airplanes between flights. HS has managers at each airport to hire, train, and supervise cleaning crews. Most crews are recent immigrants with few skills. The job pays a little above minimum wage. Part of the training emphasizes honesty, as cleaning crews frequently find cell phones, personal computers, pens, and other items left by passengers.

Some of the problems that HS struggles with are turnover, absenteeism, tardiness, and alleged theft. However, one manager, Al, has the lowest rates of turnover, absenteeism, and tardiness. He has also come to the attention of the airlines because his people regularly turn in lost articles, including wallets, credit cards, and other items of worth. HS wants their other managers to adopt some of Al's practices.

Al is very clear about what he expects of his crews in terms of being on time, showing up for work, being efficient in their tasks, and being honest. However, he discovered in talking with them some reasons why they are absent or late. He found out they had trouble finding ways to get to the airport and finding adequate childcare they could afford. He believed that as long as these were his people's problems, they were his problems as well. His solution was

- To invite representatives from the city transit authority to come to the airport and explain how his workers could get to work at the least cost using public transportation. He asked them to bring maps and be prepared to answer specific questions. They were also asked to explain how the workers might take advantage of discounts like monthly passes and where to buy the passes. He asked that they be prepared to sell passes while there.

- He asked the city's department of human services to explain how his people could apply for financial assistance for childcare and how to locate qualified sitters and day care services. He asked the representatives to bring applications and explain how to fill them out.

Another thing Al noticed was that when his workers received their first paycheck they did not understand why money was deducted for taxes. So he also invited someone from the IRS to meet with his people to discuss why taxes were withheld, how to apply for tax credits designed for people who earned less than $30,000 a year, how to determine how many eligible dependents they had, why declaring dependents was important, and how to file so they received all of the refunds they were eligible for. Prior to meeting with the IRS, most of his people did not apply for tax credits, claim the right number of dependents, or file, and, therefore, paid more than what was required and lost the opportunity to receive their refunds.

Al watched for job openings at the airport and at HS he thought his people might qualify for. He obtained applications and helped his people fill them out. He wanted his people to advance. Over time he was able to help a significant number of his people find better paying jobs. What Al received in return was a loyal and honest workforce.

The incentive for Al to come up with innovative solutions was his own performance goals. His bonus is partially dependent on his ability to control costs.

Absenteeism and turnover added unnecessary costs. The cost of giving his people time to meet with representatives from the transit authority, the city human services department, and the IRS was small compared to the cost of recruiting and training new crews.

Al's interest in helping his people solve real problems and his concern over their careers acknowledges the importance of their issues and shows them respect. His behavior has become the incentive for crews to show up daily and on time, and be honest as well. As Buckingham and Coffman say: "We had discovered that the manager—not pay, benefits, perks, or a charismatic corporate leader—was the critical player in building a strong workplace."[2]

Being courteous is perhaps one of the more significant ways managers and supervisors can recognize other people's behaviors and activities. At a minimum, people expect their managers and supervisors to demonstrate the common courtesies, like thanking them when they do something special or when they do it in a special way.

> "Effective managers are like gracious hosts and should remain polite in difficult situations. Part of graciousness is recognizing what people do. Therefore put your energy and attention into earning your people's loyalty by paying attention to those who are doing good work and focusing on their strengths. Your people owe you a job well done, but if you act like they owe it to you, you risk not getting it."[3]

At the same time, organizations should recognize those managers and supervisors who are courteous and respectful. The quality of the relationship with the boss can be a leading indicator of performance. The presence or absence of common courtesies by the supervisor or manager is a leading indicator of employee loyalty, productivity, and retention, as people identify with their bosses, not with the company.

Subordinate Behaviors

Activities and behaviors that are leading indicators of subordinates' accomplishments depend on their jobs. However, here are a few examples:

- Sales—the behaviors that lead to repeat sales and satisfied customers might be things like not promising beyond the capability of the product or the organization's capacity and capability to deliver the product or service, coming prepared for client meetings, asking for the sale, and quickly following up on customer concerns.

- Customer service—the behaviors that lead to satisfied customers might include asking permission before putting a customer on hold and explaining what you are doing during periods of silence, explaining what can and cannot be done, and giving customers options about what to do and how to do it.

- Field service technician—the behaviors that lead to lower cost of service and customer satisfaction might include arriving at the scheduled time, completing the work in one visit, documenting the work done, explaining to the customer what was done and why, and cleaning up after the work is done.

The following tool can be useful for identifying leading indicators.[4]

TOOL 8.1: HOW TO IDENTIFY LEADING INDICATORS

Purpose

The purpose of this guideline is to help you identify the behaviors and activities you want to encourage because they are leading indicators of performance. Once you have identified the behaviors or activities, you are in a better position to reinforce them by applying an appropriate incentive.

How

Together with your people and a representative from human resources:

A. Create a table similar to Figure 8.3.

B. Identify the results or outcomes that are important to your group and that affect your performance evaluation. Modify if necessary.

C. Identify and list the behaviors and activities you believe contribute to or interfere with getting results and that you want to see more of or less of on the job. Consider the behaviors in your competency statements if you have developed some.

D. Identify and list the behaviors that you and peers might engage in that would encourage the desired behaviors or discourage the ones you do not want to see.

E. Develop a list of things you might do to encourage people to engage in those behaviors and activities.

F. Define what you might promise—what rewards or recognitions you might have available—to encourage the behaviors and later acknowledge the results that occur.

Figure 8.3. Identifying Leading Indicators

Performance Goals	Possible Types of Leading Behaviors
Satisfaction • Customer Satisfaction • Customer Retention • Employee Satisfaction	Customer care behaviors Teamwork behaviors Collaboration behaviors Supervisory behaviors
Improved Performance • Product Quality • Service Quality • People Efficiency	Preparation behaviors Double-checking own work Follow-up behaviors Keeping people informed Asking for help Timeliness
Finance • Revenue • Profit • Cost Containment	Accurate calculations of costs, margins, and so on Challenging how work is done and who does it Wise use of resources Using cost-appropriate resources
Safety	Safety behaviors
Compliance	Documentation behaviors Following procedures

Hint: To identify the types of behaviors and activities you want to encourage, consider the performance measures you identified for yourself and your people. What are the behaviors or activities that are essential for producing work that satisfies the measure? Find ways to encourage those behaviors.

LAGGING INDICATORS

Lagging indicators are the accomplishments or the results that occur at a specific point in time, the end of a project, or after an implementation. The typical rewards include things like bonuses, merit increases, and promotions. Rewards of this type are frequently given out at the end of the year, the end of a performance review period, or in conjunction with a major milestone. Accomplishments can also be celebrated and acknowledged in smaller ways as well. Ideally, accomplishments are acknowledged at the time they become evident, not long after the fact. However, just focusing on results, for example, remain accident-free for six months or meet the sales quota, can produce some undesirable behaviors, particularly if there is little attention to how the results were achieved or if there is a lack of balance across the measures. Here are some examples.

SAFETY

One of the problems with incentives that focus only on staying accident-free in a high hazard work environment is that the incentive might encourage people to hide accidents. The second problem is that it encourages co-workers to exert pressure to hide injuries. A better approach is

1. To recognize and reward those workers who always wear their safety gear, follow safety procedures, stay accident-free, and identify hazards and ways to eliminate them (leading indicators).

2. To recognize and reward those supervisors who regularly conduct safety meetings in a serious way, personally inspect equipment safeguards, watch for and report on workers' safety behavior, and appropriately reprimand workers who violate safety rules (leading indicators).

The lagging indicator in this case would be to recognize supervisors whose crews are accident-free while not inflicting any environmental damage due to hazardous spills or releases.

SALES

Margin is the difference between net sales and the cost of the merchandise sold. The difference is used to cover expenses, and what is left over is the profit. If the selling price is too low, the margin is insufficient to cover expenses or allow a profit; however, if the price is too high the company risks losing sales.

One company's bonuses were solely based on total sales volume, not margin. It did not matter what the trade margin was, only the size of the sale. As a result, sales staff primarily sold at low margin independent of the size of the sale to increase their bonus, whether it helped the company or not. The result was that people received bonuses, but the company frequently lacked the cash flow to invest in improvements.

Giving out rewards based on lagging indicators works if the reward is based on meeting *all* of the goals, not just one, such as customer service, controlling costs, doing quality work, meeting production goals, and staying accident-free.

RECOGNIZING THE UNSEEN AND THE UNCLEAN

Incentive plans are usually designed for "high" performers in key positions, such as sales, production, and customer service, because it is more obvious how these jobs contribute to profits. However, it takes a lot of people to make an organization effective. Some of those people work behind the scenes and do work that is overlooked and under-appreciated, like housekeeping and maintenance. Caregivers, in particular, work in low-paying jobs, and it is assumed they are motivated by the work itself. This may be true, but they also experience emotional burnout and their efforts should be acknowledged.

THE HOMELESS SHELTER

Belinda is the manager at a homeless shelter in a major city that serves a large number of people. The shelter provides food, laundry, and bathing facilities for people who are homeless. It also provides job counseling. The shelter works on a very limited budget, so there are no funds to recognize the workers. Most people who work at the shelter came because of the rewards inherent in the job.

Belinda learned that her staff feels the Department of Human Services is a nebulous agency with a lofty mission statement that is too removed and unreal. The board that oversees the shelter sets unrealistic expectations given the magnitude of the problems of the homeless. The board is too removed to know what the front line deals with. Belinda sees it as her job to manage programs to help the homeless and to support her people as well. At one time she scheduled a fun day for her staff, but she found they could not really escape emotionally because of the magnitude of the need. There is no budget for bonuses or gifts. She feels her staff is neglected because her energy goes into scrambling for money and worrying about meeting the payroll. It is essentially impossible to close the shelter for a day so workers can receive training. What Belinda does to show her appreciation is to set up walks. Workers are encouraged to take walks, just to get away from the continuous demands of helping people in need. Belinda is quick to say "thank you" and give people a physical pat on the back. She takes a moment to let them vent their frustrations. She just listens, knowing she cannot offer any easy solutions.

THE BANK

Prior to joining the homeless shelter, Belinda was the manager of the help desk at a large city bank. At the bank, she found that little things, "at-a-boy" affirmations such as gift certificates, were more effective than money at getting people to work better. She did "take a walk days" where she took over the person's desk. She even set up ice cream days. She found these little gestures of appreciation worked because they were very personalized. Money was seen as too removed and reserved for a special echelon at the bank that Belinda's people were not members of. The people who received cash rewards were two or three levels above them. However, when Belinda received a bonus she knew it was her staff's work that made it happen. Therefore, she shared her bonus. She gave out gift certificates or hosted a catered bonus-day lunch.

MAINTENANCE

Karen is a training manager at a prestigious research facility. The scientists who work there are world-renowned. They work in modern facilities and have the latest state-of-the-art equipment in the laboratories. The scientists and their work are regularly featured in technical journals. The facility frequently hosts luncheons and receptions for the scientists.

One of the phenomena Karen noticed was that there is no budget for any recognition of the maintenance crews that keep the facilities operational. When a member of the maintenance crew earns a certification or completes an education program, there is no money for certificates, doughnuts, a luncheon, or any other type of celebration. Karen has chosen to bring luncheons she prepares herself and to send the worker's boss a personal written letter of congratulations.

Karen works in one of the older buildings with antiquated heating and plumbing that challenges even the most skilled craftsperson. During one particularly cold spell, her building temperature was never above 55 degrees for over three weeks. After many hours, the heating guy was able to solve the problem. Karen extended a hearty "thank you" and shook his hand. She said his grin was so big she feared his cheeks were going to fall off. She wrote a personal thank you to his boss. The boss, in turn, read the thank you aloud and the heating guy's co-workers gave him a round of applause. It seems no one could ever remember receiving a thank you in person or in writing before.

Take a moment to think about all the people you rely on, whether they are your direct reports or not, to do your work. Identify the little gestures you can use to acknowledge those people, especially when they do something special for you or your group.

PEER RECOGNITION

An assumption organizations make is that all recognitions and rewards must come from the boss or the organization itself. However, co-workers, customers, and team members are frequently in a better position to witness good work and reap the benefits. It is not uncommon for the manager to be removed from where the work is performed and, therefore, rarely see what people do or how they do it. Because of this phenomenon, some organizations have adopted programs that encourage peer and customer recognition. Here are some examples:

- The "I'm too clever for my job" award is given by co-workers when they see a colleague do something very clever, but not necessarily something that produced a cost savings or a process improvement. It is a piece of paper that is handed out during staff meetings. Employees and managers find it interesting to learn what others see as inventive. Ask yourself whether this type of recognition could encourage behaviors that lead to something of value, like better teamwork, improved collaboration, and trust.

- Another company allows peers to nominate co-workers for awards when they see someone receive outstanding comments from customers or do something that made a difference or led to an improvement. The person who receives the award keeps it on his or her desk until another "winner" is identified.

- A third company offered a peer award to recognize people who made a mistake and learned from it. The company valued itself as a "learning" organization and believed that mistakes were opportunities to learn. It encouraged people to admit mistakes so more people could learn from them. Unfortunately, people did not want to reveal their mistakes, so the award failed to encourage the behaviors of sharing what was learned from mistakes.

The following tool can help you to identify and select the appropriate incentives.

TOOL 8.2: HOW TO IDENTIFY AND SELECT INCENTIVES

Purpose

Here are some suggestions on what to consider and how to select an appropriate array of incentives that support the behaviors and results you want.

How

Remember, incentives come in many shapes and sizes; therefore, when looking for ways to recognize people:

A. Ask what might be meaningful to people. Just because something is meaningful to you, it may not be as meaningful to others.

B. Question whether a token of appreciation or a monetary reward will reinforce the behaviors you want or the values the company espouses.

C. Decide what you want to recognize or encourage. For example, do you want to encourage specific behaviors, reinforce the values the organization espouses, or recognize results?

D. Based on your goals, come up with a menu of options and set some guidelines for when to use them. Here are some suggestions:

   1. If you want to encourage self-responsibility for personal development:

      a. Buy and give people books, tapes, CDs, and so forth. Remind them they own them and can take them with them when they leave

      b. Model the same behavior by buying your own books and investing in your own development

2. If you want to promote professional development:

  a. Pay for conferences or membership in professional organizations

  b. Allow time for training

  c. Allow time off with pay for networking

  d. Take advantage of professional development yourself

3. If you want to recognize people's expertise:

  a. Invite them to conduct segments of a training program

  b. Ask them to do short in-service training programs for customers and colleagues

4. If you want to promote values the organization espouses such as honesty, fairness, teamwork:

  a. Consider peer and customer recognitions, as co-workers and customers are in a better position to see or be the recipient of such behaviors

  b. Model the behaviors yourself

5. If you want to encourage efficiency or quantity, recognize people who:

  a. Are able to control or remove distractions

  b. Have streamlined their work processes

6. If you want to promote quality, recognize people who:

  a. Double-check their work

  b. Find and follow industry standards

  c. Produce work that stays within equipment tolerances

  d. Use the appropriate raw materials

  E. Identify levels of rewards. For example, if your group wants a dinner at a nice restaurant if they reach their goals, what might be a lesser reward if they do not quite make it?

Hint: Consider the obvious. Recognitions, when given in earnest, do not have to be elaborate. Remember, what you do carries a lot of influence.

COMPENSATION

Compensation is an incentive. The goal is to pay people fairly. Some managers and supervisors work hard to get as much compensation for their people as possible. They want to compensate people above what they expect, so money never becomes an issue. However, employees are sometimes naïve about how much others in similar positions are compensated. Some employees perpetuate the folklore that they are underpaid. However, they fail to look at their total compensation package. Whatever your situation is, you might want to periodically remind people of what makes up their total compensation, including salary, vacation time, health benefits, matching retirement benefits, and the opportunity to set aside tax-free dollars for tuition, child or elder care, dental care, or transportation.

MEANINGFUL WORK

Perhaps the most powerful incentive to perform is the work itself, particularly if people believe what they do is important. Not all of us are in jobs that obviously contribute to society, or even to the organization's profits. It is especially important that managers and supervisors take the time to explain why jobs were created and how the organization relies on the outputs of the work. It is also important that people be challenged by the work, not see it as too easy or routine. Here's an example.

SLEEPWALKING

Sam, an engineer, had been sleepwalking through his job for about five to seven years. When his supervisor was fired, his new boss gave him lots of additional but important work. It seemed Sam's whole personality changed. He was suddenly on fire, working hard while helping others in their work. When asked what happened, he said, "When you're stuck below some unproductive dolt, it's easy to turn off." Sam said he was about to leave because his former boss was a zero and he felt his chances for progress were damned as long as he worked under him.

The challenge is to know how much work to give people so you do not burn them out emotionally or physically. Many people require meaningful work, challenges, and an acknowledgement of their mastery.

ALIGNING INCENTIVES

Since incentives are meant to recognize and reward results, it is important to identify the right combination of results and the contributing behaviors. Alignment happens when the incentive plan gets people to behave in ways that lead to desired results. Therefore, the incentive plan should be congruent with the organization's values and goals. For example, safety incentives only work when the company combines them with:

- Clear expectations about all the factors that contribute to performance, including protecting the environment, doing quality work, controlling costs, and providing good customer service
- Good documentation

The challenge is maintaining a balance across safety, environment, quality, cost, and customer service, as this example shows.

PLASTICS

At Plastics bonuses were solely based on selling at a fixed high margin. The reps were paid a salary with no commission, yet they were eligible for a bonus at the end of the year if the team sold at margin. The result of this bonus plan was that sales reps only sold small volumes because buyers of large volumes wanted price breaks. Sales reps refused to negotiate a better price because it might jeopardize their bonus. One rep recently lost a $300,000 order because she refused to lower the price.

Even though small volume sales at high margins seemed profitable, they had two negative side effects. First, they reduced the buying power with suppliers. Suppliers priced their products on volume. The long-term result was lower profits because the company could not get the price breaks it wanted. Second, salespeople do not have to be skilled at selling products, as they never had to negotiate price, overcome objections, or engage in any of the expected sales behaviors.

Sue was recently hired as an inside sales rep because of her reputation in the industry. Almost from the day she started, her sales averaged $10,000 or more, compared to the other sales reps, whose sales averaged less than $2,000. She also began to cross-sell by asking customers whether they had ordered any related merchandise. One customer called to place an order for $26,000 in plastics. Sue asked him if he had ordered the hardware and he said not yet. She asked whether she could call him back with a quote for the hardware and he agreed. Plastics didn't sell hardware, so Sue went online and found a manufacturer, negotiated a price, called the customer back and got an add-on sale of over $40,000 just for the hardware.

The new manager at Plastics wants to encourage the sales reps to be more like Sue. He wants them to take the initiative and be willing to negotiate margins with customers. To encourage the new behaviors, he offered everyone in the unit, including the warehouse workers, a $1,000 bonus if sales were higher than those of the other regions.

If you found out that your people were losing large sales, in the hundreds of thousands of dollars, because to lower the margin might jeopardize their bonus, what could you do? You could do nothing or you could document the number of lost sales. You could meet with your boss to discuss guidelines that both support the corporate mandate for a fixed margin and still allow for some flexibility for sales above a minimum amount. If you wanted your other sales reps to begin to cross-sell like Sue, you would have to redefine their jobs and come up with different performance measures. Offering everyone the same reward to encourage people to change may work the first year; however, it may not work long-term if the sales were the result of just a few people. Those people who took the initiative may feel resentment if they believe themselves to be doing all of the work, yet everyone is receiving the same reward.

In a difficult market or economic situation, employees do not want to see the organization wasting money on trinkets or doing anything that appears wasteful. In the sales world, contests are part of the culture; however, when the market is down or the economy is bad, managers should consider awards that are not seen as frivolous, as shown by this example.

CUSTOMER SERVICE AND SALES REPS

In the past the teams regularly held contests to see who had the best call-handling times, highest call volumes, and the least time between calls. The company decided to change the nature of the contests. The company wanted the contests to encourage team performance, not competitiveness between teams. One of the things the team leads did was to hold games during off-phone activities (when the call volume was low). The games focused on building and proving one's product and industry knowledge. The games were fun but work-related. Contests that were not work-related were not appreciated.

The company discovered that another one of its practices punished high performers rather than rewarding them. The best reps, those with high performance ratings, were tagged to deliver training, coach other reps, and work on special projects. However, if they were pulled out of production, their team's statistics suffered. This hurt everyone on the team, so what was thought to be recognition (being chosen to deliver training) proved to be a disincentive because of the negative effect on the team.

PROFESSIONAL STAFF

Gwen managed the department of employee relations and communications. Two of the positions that reported to her were change management experts and communications specialists. She and her staff were coordinating eleven different projects. Some of the projects were strategic in nature, as they were linked to integrating duplicate departments as the result of a merger. Every project was on a tight timeframe, and the constant balancing of all the customers' expectations was taking a toll on her people.

The company would not pay for professional development, so there was no budget for funding annual conferences. Gwen's people were well-paid and she had high expectations of them. She also believed in professional development. She wanted to encourage her people to invest in their own development and decided one way to do that was to model the behavior herself and give out books and conference tapes. When one of her people did something especially well or successfully navigated a difficult set of client demands, she gave the person a book or a tape. She always coupled it with a thank you and said, "This is yours to keep." When schedules were tight and she saw people skipping lunch, she would offer to bring in pizza or boxed lunches. Most importantly, she worked hard too. She never asked them to work harder than she did.

Recognizing professional staff can be a challenge. As in the examples above, some people may prefer recognition that helps them be more effective in their jobs or more competitive in the marketplace. So don't limit yourself to just what you might like, but ask the people. Here's a matrix to help.

TOOL 8.3: HOW TO ALIGN RECOGNITION AND REWARDS

Purpose

The purpose of these guidelines is to help you (1) identify and consider a whole array of avenues to reward or recognize performance; (2) select the most appropriate way; and (3) make sure that what you do is aligned or congruent with your organization's goals.

How

Together with your people, create a matrix similar to the one shown in Figure 8.4.

A. In the first column, list the groups of people who might receive a reward or recognition. Be sure to include direct reports, bosses, and peers.

B. In the second column, list the incentives available. You might want to list any restrictions, such as being offered annually, only one recipient annually, and so forth.

C. In the third column list what people have to do to receive an award or recognition.

D. In the fourth column list the criteria for receiving an award or recognition.

Figure 8.4. Matrix to Align Incentives

Who It Is for	What Is Available	What One Must Do	Criteria
• Direct reports • Managers • Peers	Celebrations • Lunches • Receptions Financial • Gifts • Bonuses • Merit raises Non-monitory • Email thanks • Personal notes • Certificates Development • Training • Professional dues • Time off for networking • Time off for community service	Job performance • Behaviors • Significant accomplishment • Expertise applied to real-world problems Improved system capabilities • Leadership • Mission success Corporate values • Teamwork • Outstanding people management skills • Significant use of resources • Manage risk taking • Help others succeed	• Performance or behavior having great impact • High individual performance • Short-term, high-value special assignment • Sustained level of excellence • High individual customer satisfaction • Went beyond normal job assignment • Overcame incredible odds or extenuating circumstances

This matrix is adapted from one created by a team at the Sandia National Laboratory and is offered to managers and supervisors by Charline Wells, program manager for corporate education, training, and development.

Hint: You might want to add a column or note about who can nominate a person for an award or recognition, that is, self, peer, supervisor, or customer.

TIPS

Here are some things you can do to encourage and recognize good work.

1. Draw good work to the attention of the people above you. The quality of your people's work reflects well on you, and your people will appreciate it.

2. Make the relationship between the recognition or reward and the accomplishment explicit.

3. Link all rewards to the larger goal, but customize them for different groups or individuals based on the nature of their work.

4. Keep the time between people's accomplishing a goal and receiving the recognition as short as possible.

5. Set up a private stash or create a budget for small gifts, such as gift certificates and items with the company logo on them.

6. Recognize talent and work to help your people develop it. You will get a lot of mileage and loyalty if you express interest in their careers.

7. Recognize people who do good work publicly, perhaps at meetings. If this is not possible, do it in person, preferably where the people work.

8. Remember, people will be demotivated when everyone gets a reward and it is experienced as not genuine. Rewards should never be too easy or too obvious.

9. Give gifts generously. Keep a drawer with pens, pocket knifes, travel clocks, flashlights, toolkits, and other items. Check out the internal company catalogue for new items. You want people to think, "Every time I put on the jacket, I think of you or the job I was doing."

10. Be willing to treat for pizza or bring in lunch when people are working hard to finish a project for you.

Remember what does not work:

- Unilateral, unexplained orders from top management. Get in the habit of asking for more direction. You cannot be expected to explain or support directives that you do not understand.

- Feedback on what needs to be done and what's been done wrong with no counterbalance about what was done right. Get in the habit of giving feedback frequently so you are not limited to bad news.

- Promotions that appear to favor those close to top management. You may not have any control over this, but you can still treat people with respect, do little things to acknowledge their work, and even help them pursue other employment opportunities.

- Cutting back on the perks (like reducing vacation time or raising medical deductions) while the elite enjoy installation of a gourmet coffee bar in their building so they can continue their outstanding leadership. Again, you may not control this, but you can control how you treat your people.

SUMMARY

Managers and supervisors who have good relationships with their people can beat a lousy system. Humans are amazingly resilient and can accomplish a lot if they do it passionately. However, if you have an adversarial relationship with your people, the system will win.

Look beyond the organization for rewards; come up with some yourself. Start by letting people know how important their work is and how others rely on them. Ask your people how they want to be recognized, and follow up on their suggestions.

WHERE TO LEARN MORE

The following will give you ideas for rewarding your people's performance.

Buckingham, M., and Coffman, C. *First, Break All the Rules: What the World's Greatest Managers Do Differently* (New York: Simon & Schuster, 1999). About 255 pages.

Kouzes, J.M., and Posner, B.Z. *Encouraging the Heart: A Leader's Guide to Rewarding and Recognizing Others* (San Francisco, CA: Jossey-Bass, 1999). A nice little book of about 200 pages that is full of useful ideas.

Kriegel, R. *If It Ain't Broke . . . BREAK IT* (New York: Time Warner Books, 1992).

Nelson, B. *1001 Ways to Reward Employees* (New York: Workman, 1994). About 275 pages of great ideas.

Stolovitch, H.D., and Keeps, E.J. *The Handbook of Human Performance Technology: A Comprehensive Guide for Analyzing and Solving Performance Problems in Organizations* (Silver Spring, MD: International Society for Performance Improvement, 1992). This book can be daunting on first sight; however, I encourage you to read Chapter 19 by Frances Kemmerer and Sivasailam Thiagarajan on incentive systems.

NOTES

1. Rodger Stotz, vice president, managing consultant, Maritz Inc., recommends the ideas developed by Professor Kanungo, whose research shows that for any stimuli to have motivational impact it must be (1) salient (conspicuous), (2) valued (by the recipient), and (3) contingent on performance. The specific citation is B. Kanungo and J. Hartwick, "An Alternative to the Intrinsic-Extrinsic Dichotomy of Work Rewards," *Journal of Management*, 1987, *4*, 751–756.

2. Buckingham and Coffman in *First, Break All the Rules,* page 32.

3. A quote by Donald L. Kirkey, learning and development manager, Global Operations, Johnson Controls, Inc.

4. The concept of looking at incentives in terms of leading and lagging indicators was adapted from the ideas in an article in *Occupational Health & Safety,* January 2003, pages 28–30 by Larry Bush, executive vice president, sales and marketing for Meridian Enterprises Corporation.

Index

Succeed Where Most Companies Fail), 32

N

New hire training, 122, 125
Norton, D. P. (*The Balanced Scorecard*), 32n.1

O

Oakley-Browne, H. (*Strategic Planning for Success: Aligning People, Performance, and Payoffs*), 32
Objectives: definition of, 9; in department-level goal hierarchy, 14; effects of, 11–12; hierarchy of, 13–16; identification of, 16–17; in individual-level hierarchy, 15; for learning, 124; in team-level hierarchy, 15; versus goals, 11–12
Observation, 128
Oil change case example, 143–144
Online graduate course case example, 169
On-the-job training. *See* Training
Operating guidelines, 45, 48, 51
Organizational Culture and Leadership (Schein, E.), 32–33n.2
Organizations: goal hierarchy of, 13–14; performance appraisal of, 170–171; performance indicators of, 3
Orientation: components of, 118–119; definition of, 118; guidelines for, 120–122; phases of, 118; purpose of, 119; sharing tasks of, 121–122. *See also* Training

Outcome level, of measures, 65
Outcomes: definition of, 12, 13; in department-level goal hierarchy, 14; examples of, 14, 15, 16; in individual-level hierarchy, 15; in organization-level hierarchy, 13; in team-level hierarchy, 15
Outputs. *See* Deliverables

P

Peer recognition, 190–191
People: goal hierarchy of, 15–16; indicators of good performance from, 185–186; information required by, 9; performance indicators of, 3; as point of comparison, 74; using competencies to select, 83–86. *See also* Individuals
Performance: case of poor, 156–157; definition of, 2, 58; documentation of, 156; organization's indicators of, 3; people's indicators of, 3; processes' indicators of, 3; and protocols, 44; systems' indicators of, 3
Performance appraisal: characteristics of effective, 170; components of, 171; of departments, 170; drawbacks of, 155, 170; importance of, 155–156; of individuals, 170, 171; measures for, 170–172; of organizations, 170–171; purpose of, 170; types of, 171; unfair, 172; versus feedback, 170. *See also* Evaluation

About the Author

J udith Hale, CPT, has dedicated her career to helping management professionals develop effective, practical ways to improve individual and organizational performance. She has used the techniques, processes, and job aids described in this book in her own consulting work, which has spanned twenty-five years. Judith's clients speak of the practicality of her approach and the proven results it yields. She is able to explain complex ideas so that people understand their relevance and can apply them to their own situations. She is able to help others come to a shared understanding about what to do and how to commit to action.

Her consulting firm, Hale Associates, was founded in 1974 and enjoys long-term relationships with a variety of major corporations. The services her firm provides include consultation on alignment, assessment, certification, evaluation, integration of performance improvement systems, performance management, and strategic planning.

She is the author of *The Performance Consultant's Fieldbook, Performance-Based Evaluation,* and *Performance-Based Certification.* Her book *Achieving a Leadership Role for Training* describes how training can apply the standards espoused by the International Standards Organization and Baldrige to its own operation. She was the topic editor for *Designing Work Groups, Jobs, and Work Flow* and for *Designing Cross-Functional Business Processes* and the author of the chapter "The Hierarchy of Interventions" in the *Sourcebook for Performance Improvement.* Judith also wrote *The Training Manager Competencies: The Standards,* as well as *The Training Function Standards* and *Standards for Qualifying Trainers,* and she put together the *Workbook and Job Aids for Good Fair Tests,* and was a contributor to *What Smart Trainers Know,* edited by Lorraine Ukens (2001, Jossey-Bass/Pfeiffer).

Judith is an appointed member of the Illinois Occupational Skills Standard and Credentialing Council. She is a past president of the International Society for Performance Improvement (ISPI) and of the Chicago chapter of the National Society of Performance and Instruction (NSPI) and has served on NSPI's President's Advisory Council. NSPI named her Outstanding Member of the Year in 1987. She has also served as president of the International Board of Standards for Performance and Instruction and president of the Chicago chapter of the Industrial Relations Research Association (IRRA). She was a commercial arbitrator with the American Arbitration Association and has been a member of the American Society for Training and Development (ASTD) for many years. She was nominated for ASTD's Gordon Bliss Award in 1995. She taught graduate courses in management for fourteen years for the Insurance School of Chicago and received the school's Outstanding Educator award in 1986.

Judith speaks regularly at ASTD International, ASTD Technical Skills, the International Society for Performance Improvement, and Lakewood's annual training conferences.

Judith holds a B.A. from Ohio State University (communication), an M.A. from Miami University (theater management), and a Ph.D. from Purdue University (instructional design, with minors in organizational communication and adult education). She has received the International Society for Performance Improvement's certification, Certified Performance Technologist.

How to Use the CD-ROM

SYSTEM REQUIREMENTS

- PC with Microsoft Windows 98SE or later
- Mac with Apple OS version 8.6 or later
- CD-ROM Drive

USING THE CD WITH WINDOWS

To view the items located on the CD, follow these steps:

1. Insert the CD into your computer's CD-ROM drive.

2. A window appears with the following options:

    Contents: Allows you to view the files included on the CD-ROM.
    Software: Allows you to install useful software from the CD-ROM.
    Links: Displays a hyperlinked page of Web sites.
    Author: Displays a page with information about the Author(s).
    Contact Us: Displays a page with information on contacting the publisher or Help: Displays a page with information on using the CD.
    Exit: Closes the interface window.

If you do not have autorun enabled, or if the autorun window does not appear, follow these steps to access the CD:

1. Click Start -> Run.

2. In the dialog box that appears, type d:\start.exe, where d is the letter of your CD-ROM drive. This brings up the autorun window described in the preceding set of steps.

3. Choose the desired option from the menu. (See Step 2 in the preceding list for a description of these options.)

IN CASE OF TROUBLE

If you experience difficulty using the CD-ROM, please follow these steps:

1. Make sure your hardware and systems configurations conform to the systems requirements noted under "System Requirements" above.

2. Review the installation procedure for your type of hardware and operating system. It is possible to reinstall the software if necessary.

To speak with someone in Product Technical Support, call 800-762-2974 or 317-572-3994 M–F 8:30 a.m.–5:00 p.m. EST. You can also get support and contact Product Technical Support through our website at http://www.wiley.com/techsupport.

Before calling or writing, please have the following information available:

- Type of computer and operating system
- Any error messages displayed
- Complete description of the problem.

It is best if you are sitting at your computer when making the call. Windows PC

Pfeiffer Publications Guide

This guide is designed to familiarize you with the various types of Pfeiffer publications. The formats section describes the various types of products that we publish; the methodologies section describes the many different ways that content might be provided within a product. We also provide a list of the topic areas in which we publish.

FORMATS

In addition to its extensive book-publishing program, Pfeiffer offers content in an array of formats, from fieldbooks for the practitioner to complete, ready-to-use training packages that support group learning.

FIELDBOOK Designed to provide information and guidance to practitioners in the midst of action. Most fieldbooks are companions to another, sometimes earlier, work, from which its ideas are derived; the fieldbook makes practical what was theoretical in the original text. Fieldbooks can certainly be read from cover to cover. More likely, though, you'll find yourself bouncing around following a particular theme, or dipping in as the mood, and the situation, dictate.

HANDBOOK A contributed volume of work on a single topic, comprising an eclectic mix of ideas, case studies, and best practices sourced by practitioners and experts in the field.

An editor or team of editors usually is appointed to seek out contributors and to evaluate content for relevance to the topic. Think of a handbook not as a ready-to-eat meal, but as a cookbook of ingredients that enables you to create the most fitting experience for the occasion.

RESOURCE Materials designed to support group learning. They come in many forms: a complete, ready-to-use exercise (such as a game); a comprehensive resource on one topic (such as conflict management) containing a variety of methods and approaches; or a collection of like-minded activities (such as icebreakers) on multiple subjects and situations.

TRAINING PACKAGE An entire, ready-to-use learning program that focuses on a particular topic or skill. All packages comprise a guide for the facilitator/trainer and a workbook for the participants. Some packages are supported with additional media—such as video—or learning aids, instruments, or other devices to help participants understand concepts or practice and develop skills.

- *Facilitator/trainer's guide* Contains an introduction to the program, advice on how to organize and facilitate the learning event, and step-by-step instructor notes. The guide also contains copies of presentation materials—handouts, presentations, and overhead designs, for example—used in the program.

- *Participant's workbook* Contains exercises and reading materials that support the learning goal and serves as a valuable reference and support guide for participants in the weeks and months that follow the learning event. Typically, each participant will require his or her own workbook.

ELECTRONIC CD-ROMs and web-based products transform static Pfeiffer content into dynamic, interactive experiences. Designed to take advantage of the searchability, automation, and ease-of-use that technology provides, our e-products bring convenience and immediate accessibility to your workspace.

METHODOLOGIES

CASE STUDY A presentation, in narrative form, of an actual event that has occurred inside an organization. Case studies are not prescriptive, nor are they used to prove a point; they are designed to develop critical analysis and decision-making skills. A case study has a specific time frame, specifies a sequence of events, is narrative in structure, and contains a plot structure—an issue (what should be/have been done?). Use case studies when the goal is to enable participants to apply previously learned theories to the circumstances in the case, decide what is pertinent, identify the real issues, decide what should have been done, and develop a plan of action.

ENERGIZER A short activity that develops readiness for the next session or learning event. Energizers are most commonly used after a break or lunch to stimulate or refocus the group. Many involve some form of physical activity, so they are a useful way to counter post-lunch lethargy. Other uses include transitioning from one topic to another, where "mental" distancing is important.

EXPERIENTIAL LEARNING ACTIVITY (ELA) A facilitator-led intervention that moves participants through the learning cycle from experience to application (also known as a Structured Experience). ELAs are carefully thought-out designs in which there is a definite learning purpose and intended outcome. Each step—everything that participants do during the activity—facilitates the accomplishment of the stated goal. Each ELA includes complete instructions for facilitating the intervention and a clear statement of goals, suggested group size and timing, materials required, an explanation of the process, and, where appropriate, possible variations to the activity. (For more detail on Experiential Learning Activities, see the Introduction to the *Reference Guide to Handbooks and Annuals*, 1999 edition, Pfeiffer, San Francisco.)

GAME A group activity that has the purpose of fostering team spirit and togetherness in addition to the achievement of a pre-stated goal. Usually contrived—undertaking a desert expedition, for example—this type of learning method offers an engaging means for participants to demonstrate and practice business and interpersonal skills. Games are effective for team building and personal development mainly because the goal is subordinate to the process—the means through which participants reach decisions, collaborate, communicate, and generate trust and understanding. Games often engage teams in "friendly" competition.

ICEBREAKER A (usually) short activity designed to help participants overcome initial anxiety in a training session and/or to acquaint the participants with one another. An icebreaker can be a fun activity or can be tied to specific topics or training goals. While a useful tool in itself, the icebreaker comes into its own in situations where tension or resistance exists within a group.

INSTRUMENT A device used to assess, appraise, evaluate, describe, classify, and summarize various aspects of human behavior. The term used to describe an instrument depends primarily on its format and purpose. These terms include survey, questionnaire, inventory, diagnostic, survey, and poll. Some uses of instruments include providing instrumental feedback to group members, studying here-and-now processes or functioning within a group, manipulating group composition, and evaluating outcomes of training and other interventions.

Instruments are popular in the training and HR field because, in general, more growth can occur if an individual is provided with a method for focusing specifically on his or her own behavior. Instruments also are used to obtain information that will serve as a basis for change and to assist in workforce planning efforts.

Paper-and-pencil tests still dominate the instrument landscape with a typical package comprising a facilitator's guide, which offers advice on administering the instrument and interpreting the collected data, and an initial set of instruments. Additional instruments are available separately. Pfeiffer, though, is investing heavily in e-instruments. Electronic instrumentation provides effortless distribution and, for larger groups particularly, offers advantages over paper-and-pencil tests in the time it takes to analyze data and provide feedback.

LECTURETTE A short talk that provides an explanation of a principle, model, or process that is pertinent to the participants' current learning needs. A lecturette is intended to establish a common language bond between the trainer and the participants by providing a mutual frame of reference. Use a lecturette as an introduction to a group activity or event, as an interjection during an event, or as a handout.

MODEL A graphic depiction of a system or process and the relationship among its elements. Models provide a frame of reference and something more tangible, and more easily remembered, than a verbal explanation. They also give participants something to "go on," enabling them to track their own progress as they experience the dynamics, processes, and relationships being depicted in the model.

ROLE PLAY A technique in which people assume a role in a situation/scenario: a customer service rep in an angry-customer exchange, for example. The way in which the role is approached is then discussed and feedback is offered. The role play is often repeated using a different approach and/or incorporating changes made based on feedback received. In other words, role playing is a spontaneous interaction involving realistic behavior under artificial (and safe) conditions.

SIMULATION A methodology for understanding the interrelationships among components of a system or process. Simulations differ from games in that they test or use a model that depicts or mirrors some aspect of reality in form, if not necessarily in content. Learning occurs by studying the effects of change on one or more factors of the model. Simulations are commonly used to test hypotheses about what happens in a system—often referred to as "what if?" analysis—or to examine best-case/worst-case scenarios.

THEORY A presentation of an idea from a conjectural perspective. Theories are useful because they encourage us to examine behavior and phenomena through a different lens.

TOPICS

The twin goals of providing effective and practical solutions for workforce training and organization development and meeting the educational needs of training and human resource professionals shape Pfeiffer's publishing program. Core topics include the following:

Leadership & Management

Communication & Presentation

Coaching & Mentoring

Training & Development

E-Learning

Teams & Collaboration

OD & Strategic Planning

Human Resources

Consulting